RAISING A HIGHLY SENSITIVE CHILD

How To Help Our Exceptionally Persistent Kids Flourish Including Meltdown Tips and Tricks

© Copyright 2021 - All rights reserved.

The content contained within this book may not be reproduced, duplicated or transmitted without direct written permission from the author or the publisher.

Under no circumstances will any blame or legal responsibility be held against the publisher, or author, for any damages, reparation, or monetary loss due to the information contained within this book, either directly or indirectly.

Legal Notice:

This book is copyright protected. It is only for personal use. You cannot amend, distribute, sell, use, quote or paraphrase any part, or the content within this book, without the consent of the author or publisher.

Disclaimer Notice:

Please note the information contained within this document is for educational and entertainment purposes only. All effort has been executed to present accurate, up to date, reliable, complete information. No warranties of any kind are declared or implied. Readers acknowledge that the author is not engaging in the rendering of legal, financial, medical or professional advice. The content within this book has been derived from various sources. Please consult a licensed professional before attempting any techniques outlined in this book.

By reading this document, the reader agrees that under no circumstances is the author responsible for any losses, direct or indirect, that are incurred as a result of the use of information contained within this document, including, but not limited to, errors, omissions, or inaccuracies.

TABLE OF CONTENTS

RAISING A HIGHLY SENSITIVE CHILD.........1

Introduction 5

Chapter 1: Understanding and Recognizing a Highly Sensitive Child 11
Definition of a HSC (Highly Sensitive Child) 17
What It Means to Be an Introvert......................21

Chapter 2: Nature of Sensitivity 27
Nature of Sensitivity...29
Different Types of Highly Sensitive Personalities 30

Chapter 3: Is Your Child Spoiled or Sensitive? 41

Chapter 4: Disorders Linked to the HSC...............52

Chapter 5: Understanding the Beauty of HS in Children...63
The Beauty in Highly Sensitive Children 65
Why Their Emotions Make Them Excellent Listeners..71

Chapter 6: Dealing with Externalities Part 1: Environmental Sensitivities..................................75

Why It's Important to Deal with Environmental Sensitivities 76

Important Things to Remember 86

Chapter 7: Dealing with Externalities Part 2: Relationships 89

What You Shouldn't Do 100

Chapter 8: Dealing with Externalities Part 3: Typical Routines 102

The Importance of Daily Routines 103

Typical Routines 105

Chapter 9: Meltdown Tips and Tricks 115

Earth Elements 122

Chapter 10: Disciplining a Highly Sensitive Child 130

Disciplining an HSC 132

Reflect on Yourself 134

Things to Avoid 141

Things to Do 141

Conclusion 144

References 148

INTRODUCTION

Raising a highly sensitive child is an incredibly difficult task for any parent. They tend to be exceptionally aware of everything around them and will react quickly to any stimuli. Highly sensitive children experience emotions on a deeper level than others, having the capacity for great empathy and perceiving their surroundings very acutely. They can also be strong-willed, pressing an issue until they get their way. While these are usually positive traits in an adult, it can be extraordinarily overwhelming for a child, and this often leads to them exhibiting behavioral problems that aren't always easy to manage.

Coping with Highly Sensitive Children

There are some great strategies you can employ to deal with highly sensitive children. Before you even start to try to cope with your child's outbursts, you need to get a handle on your own emotions. This is particularly important if your child is having a meltdown due to your decisions, such as telling them they can't go somewhere or do something they wanted to do. Our natural instinct as human beings is to become defensive, but this will only end up escalating the problem. It's also imperative not to simply give in to your child because it seems like the easiest way to bring the situation to a close. Take a deep breath and keep yourself from making any rash remarks or decisions. This way, you can think clearly before you start dealing with your child's issues.

Show Your Child Empathy

When your child is having an outburst or throwing a temper tantrum, you need to demonstrate that you empathize with them. Tell them that you understand why they are feeling the way they do. Don't simply walk away from the situation and hope that they will calm down on their own. This can send a message that they aren't accepted and cause even more behavioral problems with them in the future. You need to acknowledge their feelings and allow them the chance to express to you why they feel that way.

Set Boundaries and Be Direct

After you've established communication with your child and demonstrated that you understand the problem, you must set boundaries that you're willing to follow through on. Your child needs to see consistency in your behavior, so giving him/her a predictable set of boundaries that don't change will instill in them the sense that they can depend on you, even if they don't realize it at the moment. You also need to make sure they understand why you've set these boundaries and explain to them the reasons for their consequences. This is how they learn from your disciplinary measures, rather than simply being punished without grasping the correlation between their actions and the repercussions. When they understand consequences, it makes the whole experience easier for them and for you.

Use the Right Tone

It's necessary to utilize the right tone when you discipline your child in order to have a more effective outcome. You have to speak firmly but with warmth and understanding. Talking to them in a calm and respectful manner will be far more effective than taking on an authoritarian voice. Your child feeds off your tone and will react to you accordingly. If you show them you understand and respect them as an individual, they are more likely to do the same.

Strategies in Action

I have a highly sensitive child, a six-year-old named Teddy. Teddy cries a lot and is often getting his feelings hurt over seemingly minor issues. In school, he is fairly well-liked, but if another child doesn't want to play with him for some reason, it makes him feel like nobody wants to be his friend. He will come home and spend the night fretting about whether or not the other children will be his friends when he returns to school the next day. This leads to him having meltdowns about it before going to bed.

In order to deal with these problems, I employed strategies for dealing with a highly sensitive child. When Teddy had an outburst, crying hysterically as I was getting him ready for bed, I calmly told him that I knew what he was going through. I explained in an empathetic manner that people don't always feel like doing the same things we do, but it doesn't mean they don't like us. I also explained that the child who didn't want to play with him may have simply wanted to do something else or could have been in a bad mood and simply wanted to be left alone.

I assured Teddy that this doesn't mean the child doesn't want to be his friend, and it isn't indicative of Teddy's appeal as a person. I made sure Teddy knew that he is a very special and likable person, and he has plenty of friends at school. Even if that one child didn't want to be his friend, that's okay. Everyone is different, and sometimes certain people just don't mesh. However, I told Teddy that this is okay, and it's okay not to be friends with everyone. He still has plenty of other great friends that he can have fun playing with. This calmed Teddy down, and he was able to remember this the next time there was an issue with the other child in school.

Get Started Early

The earlier in your child's development that you employ these strategies, the better they will work and make it easier for you to manage them. Children begin forming habits and neurological connections between their emotions and behavior at a very young age. If you wait too long to deal with them in the right way, it can become much more difficult to create good habits and give your child stability in your interactions with them. Starting early with these strategies will make it easier to manage their severe emotional states and let you build a better relationship with them.

To truly learn how to deal with a highly sensitive child, there are many aspects of their behavior and management tools you must become familiar with. This book will give you those tools so you can have an easier and more productive relationship with your child. By the end, you'll have everything you need to properly raise your highly sensitive child.

CHAPTER 1:

UNDERSTANDING AND RECOGNIZING A HIGHLY SENSITIVE CHILD

Many parents of highly sensitive children don't recognize that their children are highly sensitive from the beginning, which causes a lot of stress and confusion as they just don't get it. Moreover, the stress added by others when they start commenting on their children's reactions or looking at them in a way that means you spoil your kid, and you are the reason behind their behavior makes these parents feel guilty.

Parents are not the only ones involved in raising and disciplining highly sensitive children, as teachers are involved too. When teachers are unaware that they have a highly sensitive child in their class and see their reactions are different from their classmates, they wonder if they are doing the right thing for this student or not. Moreover, there are many cases where teachers have thought that a highly sensitive child has attention difficulties or is not motivated enough, simply because of the lack of awareness about HSC.

When parents or teachers feel unable to support their children or students or put their hands on the problem, they feel guilty and frustrated. Moreover, the children do not get the support they need to reach their potential as they are constantly misunderstood and pushed to do things that overwhelms them and drain their energies. However, high sensitivity is not a disorder. It is a temperament type that needs to be identified and understood to be able to provide these children with the support they need to help them understand and develop their emotions in a healthy way to become happy, confident adults.

Some biologists perceive high sensitivity as an evolutionary advantage as high sensitivity is not limited to humans. There are about 100 highly sensitive species other than humans. Moreover, highly sensitive people are more connected to the environment and see things others usually miss or ignore. Also, highly sensitive people have very strong intuition and are able to make smart decisions even in very unusual situations.

Fifteen to twenty percent of children born are highly sensitive children, and in a favorable environment, they score higher grades than their classmates, have better moral attitudes, have higher levels of self-regulation, and feel more secure when they get the love and support of their families. It is very important to know that your child or student doesn't need to be fixed, and there is no set clinical diagnosis for high sensitivity as it is not a disorder. However, it is very important to understand and recognize highly sensitive children to help them to cope with the environment and achieve their full potential. Here are some of the most common traits displayed by highly sensitive children:

Take in More Sensory Information

Highly sensitive children take in more sensory information from their surrounding environment than other children. They are able to hear faint sounds and detect subtle smells. Also, they notice details other children miss, like details in drawings, for example. They can be sensitive to certain fabrics, and they hate to wear them, and even with food, they can find a flavor too strong for their taste.

Process Information Thoroughly

Highly sensitive children have a deeply reflective inner life. Therefore, they are creative and intuitive. They also pick up on things other children of the same age don't.

They Are Empaths

They have strong empathy for others and can feel their sadness and happiness all the same. Highly sensitive children are emotional and take on the emotions of other people around them, and feel strongly about what they feel.

They Are Easily Overstimulated

Highly sensitive children get tired easily and need rest more often than other children their age.

They Are Prone to Sudden Meltdowns

Since they are very sensitive to their surroundings and their environment, they can get overwhelmed by all the emotions, sounds, and information. That is why they are prone to sudden tantrums and meltdowns. Places that you might think are fun for them can become too much for them.

Moreover, highly sensitive children don't like to participate in discussions or activities. For example, a highly sensitive student would be reluctant to answer in class. They always stand out even if they are not overly active or demanding. Highly sensitive children like predictability; that is why they worry a lot, even about fun activities like trips and Christmas gatherings, to the point that their worry can manifest itself in physical pain like headaches or stomach aches. Therefore, sometimes people label them as shy or anxious children who can't adapt to little changes in life. However, instead of these labels, we can describe highly sensitive children as children with a strong sense of caution, consequences and who are highly conscientious. These are the three C's of highly sensitive children. Let us dig deeper into them;

1. Strong Sense of Caution

Highly sensitive children have a very active behavioral inhibition system. When put in a situation, they check within themselves and see if this situation is similar to a past situation they have experienced before. Moreover, if a highly sensitive child is forced into an unfamiliar or new situation, chances are they will not enjoy it and will protest or refuse it altogether. For them, new experiences are like a flood of new sensory experiences. Highly sensitive children aren't really poor adaptors, but they are constantly asked to adapt to a lot of changes. Before a highly sensitive child can relax, they need to process all new stimulations, which is why this kind of pressure makes them overwhelmed.

2. Strong Sense of Consequences

As mentioned above, highly sensitive children are more mature than children their age. Therefore, unlike other children, they are aware of the consequences of their actions and the impact of external factors on them. Thus, they try to avoid any risks of negative consequences. For example, if a highly sensitive child heard on the news that there was a fire somewhere which caused damage, they would worry about their safety and ask about the safety measures in their home in order to feel safe.

3. Highly Sensitive Children Are Highly Conscientious

A highly sensitive child always wants to do the right thing. They are highly continuous, and they take personal mistakes hard. Highly sensitive children can't get over embarrassment easily. Moreover, they are hard on themselves because making mistakes is perceived as if they are inadequate. Thus, they don't like situations or events with risks of making mistakes, especially in public like recitals, exams, and, of course, public speaking.

Definition of a HSC (Highly Sensitive Child)

Highly sensitive children have a nervous system that is highly aware and quick to react to everything. They notice small changes around them quickly and tend to reflect before they act deeply. In general, highly sensitive children behave conscientiously. They are described as easily prone to stress, reactive, and shy. If there is a high level of simulation, a sudden change, or someone in front of them is emotionally distressed, they feel overwhelmed. However, not all highly sensitive children have the same exact traits as some are a bit difficult- active, demanding, and emotionally intense - while others are calm and tend to turn inward except when asked to join a group of children they don't know. Therefore, they can have different personality traits, but all of them are sensitive to their emotional and physical environment.

Why Is My Child Highly Sensitive?

Research suggests that high sensitivity is genetic. However, it is not related to one gene, particularly as studies have shown that personality traits are formed based on several genes. At least three separate sets of genes may be one of the reasons behind high sensitivity. However, only one of these genes can affect the brain or the nervous system. Highly sensitive children may have all of these genes or only some of them. These three sets of genes are Serotonin Transporter, Dopamine Genes, and a gene related to Norepinephrine.

Serotonin Transporter

Serotonin is a chemical in the body that is responsible for many things, and one of them is stabilizing our mood. The Serotonin transporter is another chemical that is responsible for transporting serotonin out of the brain. It is kind of an on and off switch for Serotonin. Researchers have found that highly sensitive people have a special variation of the serotonin transporter gene, and they act in a somehow different way. Children with these gene variants (5-HTTLPR) have lower serotonin levels, which increases the chances that they will become highly sensitive. People used to believe that this gene variant causes depression, but that is not true as it cannot cause any mood disorder on its own. However, it is responsible for making a person sensitive to their surroundings. So, if you add an unhealthy childhood to this gene, you get an increased risk of depression and other disorders.

On the other hand, add a safe, secure, and supportive environment to children who have this gene, and you get a happy person who knows how to cope with their high sensitivity and turn it into a positive state, like becoming creative, unconventional thinkers. Remember, high sensitivity is not a disorder, and highly sensitive children do not need to be fixed. It is a temperament that needs to be recognized and understood.

The Dopamine Genes

Scientists are not a hundred percent sure that dopamine genes are related to high sensitivity. However, researchers say there are some signs that there are some connections between high sensitivity and a set of 10 different gene variants related to dopamine. Since dopamine is called the reward chemical, it makes sense that a highly sensitive child doesn't want to feel rewarded by an external stimulus because they will get back to that stimulus in the loud environment that exhausts them. Maybe that is why highly sensitive children do not enjoy loud birthday parties and aggressive games because they do not have the same dopamine hit from them as other children of their age.

The Gene Related to the Norepinephrine

Norepinephrine is a neurotransmitter that helps with the way the body responds to stress. There is a gene variant that controls the way people respond to emotional moments and situations. This one variant may be common in highly sensitive children as they are more emotional than other children, and their reactions to emotional situations are stronger. Also, highly sensitive children are empaths and aware of other's feelings. Thus, there may be a link between highly sensitive children and the norepinephrine gene variant.

High sensitivity in children is not a negative trait at all. On the contrary, if you accept your child/student the way they are and acknowledge their needs, they will excel in their life. Highly sensitive children are very creative, and when they are provided with the needed support, they can add so much to their community. They are out-of-the-box thinkers who are able to stand out with their creative ideas and resolutions.

What It Means to Be an Introvert

Note that not all highly sensitive children are introverts. However, they are more likely to be introverts than extroverts. Although highly sensitive children and introverts have some traits in common, they are not the same.

Introverts

Introverts cope with the world by internal thinking and do not focus on social connections. Sights and sounds can cause an overwhelming sensation to introverts, and that is why they try to limit their experiences. However, being an introverted child doesn't necessarily mean that they are shy or unsociable, as many introverts are social children and enjoy spending time with a few of their friends. They just need to spend much time alone to recharge, so they can face the world again as they get drained faster than others.

HSC is related to genes, so it is genetic. Their brains process dopamine in a different way than other children. Highly sensitive children and introverted children do not feel rewarded by external stimuli like big birthday parties and so on. On the other hand, introverts enjoy meaningful activities, so you will find them enjoying reading as much as performing creative hobbies. Unlike highly sensitive children, introverts don't have to be highly sensitive. They are not as stressed by time pressure or aggressive games, for example, as highly sensitive children are. Moreover, highly sensitive children are empaths, but not all introverts are empaths. However, it makes sense that quite often, people can't differentiate between highly sensitive children and introverts.

Typically, introverted children:

- Are good listeners.

- Need their time to think and ponder before they answer.

- Need more alone time to recharge.

- Most probably won't share their emotions.

- Are observant.

- Are very aware of themselves.

- Highly regard inner reflection.

- Prefer one-on-one communication.

If your child is an introvert, then that is their nature, and it is not going to change. Unless your child is showing signs of depression or anxiety, then you do not need to worry. Embrace the nature of your child and accept that they do not have to enjoy the events and things that other children do.

As a parent of an introverted child, there are some points that you need to acknowledge so that both of you can accept the differences and enjoy a rewarding life;

- Many successful and famous people around the world are introverts, and there is nothing weird or shameful about being an introvert.

- Most introverted and extroverted brains do not use the same pathways of neurotransmitters, and unlike extroverts, introverts prefer the parasympathetic side of the nervous system. Therefore, introverts will stay introverts, and there is nothing wrong with that.

- Although introverts get anxious in new environments or when they meet new people, they will gradually open up to them as they get more familiar. They just need their time, and that is okay.

- Pushing your child to socialize and trying to take them out a lot to "fix" their introverted behavior will drain their energy.

- When your child decides to take the risk of getting to know new people, encourage them and praise their courage.

- It is very important that parents of introverted children realize that their children tend to internalize their problems, so you need to ask them in a nice way and listen to them attentively.

- Your child loves you. They just get drained by anything that takes them out of their inner world. Do not get upset when your child chooses to spend more time alone. They love you and enjoy spending time with you, but they need to recharge.

- Your child is perfect the way he or she is. There is nothing scary or wrong with being an introvert. They just enjoy life in a different way.

- Introverted children may have unique hobbies and interests. Give them a chance to express themselves in a creative way.

- Parents of introverted children need to let teachers at school know that their children are introverts because some teachers assume that they don't like to participate because they are not paying attention.

- Teach your child to stand up for themselves as introverted children may find it hard to say no or stand up for themselves.

- As a parent, you need to understand that your child lives internally, and you need to draw them out to know what they are thinking about. Help your children to express and talk about their emotions and thoughts with you.

CHAPTER 2: NATURE OF SENSITIVITY

Raising a highly sensitive child can be quite tiring, but, at the same time, it can also be a very rewarding experience. As a parent of a highly sensitive child, you need to understand that no parenting strategy will work with every sensitive child. Every child is unique, and, as a parent, you will, over time, have to develop your unique approach. But to do so, it is essential that you understand what sensitivity means. When can you say that your child is highly sensitive? Is it when your child gets bothered by bright lights and loud noises? Or is it when your child demonstrates insatiable curiosity, following up one question with the next? Nearly one child in every 5 children is born with a nervous system that is more responsive, highly aware, and quicker to react to changes and factors, both internal and external. These children, blessed with a more sensitive nervous system, can be extremely perceptive and responsive to their surroundings, be it the lighting, smell, sound, or even the mood of the people around them.

Highly sensitive children are often categorized as shy and emotional, and their high sensitivity can often make it more challenging for them to navigate the ins and outs of daily life. But the first thing that you must realize is that being a highly sensitive person is neither a medical condition nor is it a problem. It is not something that must be treated or looked down upon.

Being highly sensitive is a personality trait and more of a boon than being a bane. Some children are affected by bright lights and sounds and may prefer to read comic books and engage in quiet games over participating in sports. Some, on the other hand, may be highly energetic, engaging in a lot of sports and physical activities. Some children could be extremely inquisitive and intelligent and will excel in academics. Being highly sensitive has its benefits, and highly sensitive children are often gifted and talented intellectually, emotionally, and creatively. But they can often find it difficult to deal with large crowds and respond to new, different, and unfamiliar situations. They can easily get distracted and uncomfortable due to loud noises, and their reaction may be demonstrated in socially unacceptable ways. The emotional distress of others can bother them. But, at the same time, they understand the feelings of others better than their peers, and they are generally more considerate and capable of empathizing with others. They also have the capacity to demonstrate courage and are more inclined to become leaders, hold their stand and fight for what is right.

Nature of Sensitivity

Not all highly sensitive children are the same. In fact, there are different types of sensitivities that children are blessed with and experience in their day-to-day lives. As a parent, it is crucial for you to identify the nature of the sensitivity your child displays. That will probably be your most important step toward becoming a better parent. While being highly sensitive is not a problem and is rather a personality trait, as a parent, it is important that you understand that highly sensitive children require extra care, affection, understanding, motivation, and emotional support. Most of all, you will need a lot of patience. They should be taught and guided to see and identify their sensitivity, not as their weakness, but as their strength, to be able to take advantage of their talents, skills, and empathy. Accepting and embracing your child as being highly sensitive is the first step. Only once you embrace the sensitivities of your child will you be able to push them forward rather than try and subdue their sensitivity, which could be counterproductive.

Understanding the nature of sensitivity of your child can help you adapt your parenting methodology and understand how to respond in different situations. Highly sensitive children exhibit a higher propensity to grasp new concepts and do well academically, provided they are offered a conducive and supportive environment. While the path to raising a strong-willed, highly sensitive child may not be very straightforward but instead be rather challenging if the right approach is taken and ample love, support, and compassion are provided, they will respond better than their peers, and the experience will be extremely gratifying.

Different Types of Highly Sensitive Personalities

There are different types of highly sensitive personalities, and understanding them can help you understand what kind of parenting approach would be the best one for your child. But while there are different natures of sensitivities, many of them are interrelated, and although they may not be independent of each other, your child could display them in varying degrees.

Emotional

Emotional sensitivity in children is often seen in different forms and can make it easier or difficult for children to respond and deal with emotional situations. Emotional sensitivity is generally measured on two different scales. The first scale describes how sensitive the children are and how well they understand the emotions and feelings of others. Some children tend to be unresponsive to the emotions that they see around them, while others are not only in tune with them but are also affected by the emotions of people around them. While the first scale measures how well children understand the emotions of others, the second scale measures how well they understand their own emotions. Highly sensitive children tend to be more in tune with their feelings. They understand their emotions and feel things very deeply. Less sensitive children are often unaware of their feelings. These two scales are often used to identify if a child is highly sensitive emotionally.

Emotionally sensitive children generally display a higher tendency to express emotions like anger, happiness, sorry, and embarrassment, and they often tend to do it more dramatically than others. This is a result of their being more in tune with their feelings than other children. It is thus important to understand this aspect of their behavior and respond appropriately by not telling them to suppress their feelings but instead teaching and guiding them on how to respond and express their feelings in an acceptable manner. In addition to understanding their feelings, their sensitivity toward the emotions of others makes them more sympathetic, empathetic, and courteous toward others. On the other hand, children who are emotionally less sensitive can also often find it difficult to adapt to social situations and may often appear to be rude and cold.

The Orchid Child

Children are often stressed by both small and major changes in life. The first day of school, moving to a new house, and even social issues like fighting with friends. While all children find it difficult to adjust to stressful situations, some children are affected worse than others. Most children, over time, learn to adapt and adjust to changes around them with time. They are like dandelions and adapt to changes in their environment and learn to thrive and survive. However, highly sensitive children are like orchids and can have a stronger and more adverse response. When they are exposed to stress, they tend to have a long and drawn-out response. This can result in cortisol levels that remain high for a longer duration and can lead to other problems. While highly sensitive children tend to be more affected by stress and pressure, they also have a higher capacity of responding to positive, stimulating, and supportive environments.

Identifying if your child is an orchid child is thus very important to be able to nurture them and guide them in the right direction. But what exactly are the defining characteristics of an orchid child? An Orchid Child tends to have stronger neurobiological responses to stressors than their peers. They tend to be shy and introverted and are often extremely sensitive to particular sounds, smells, and tastes. Certain things will often startle them and make them uncomfortable, things that we would take in our stride. An untidy bed, a wrinkled shirt, unfinished sentences, and other things like these can often trouble an orchid child. The behavior of an orchid child is often influenced by early experiences, although genes play an important role as well.

Intellectual

Highly sensitive children demonstrate a variety of traits. One of the traits they tend to exhibit is the ability to understand and absorb their surroundings much better than other children. In addition to often being more emotional and empathetic than their peers, they often have a higher capacity to absorb information and are able to focus and be creative. These children are gifted intellectually and will often process things more deeply and respond with unusual, effective, and creative ideas. But at the same time, they respond poorly to pressure and stress and are not very good at dealing with deadlines. But the biggest indicator of some children being intellectually sensitive and gifted is their inquisitiveness and their evident curiosity. They will constantly ask questions about different things, how things work, and why certain things are the way they are. They will also tend to score higher on IQ tests as well.

If your child is intellectually sensitive, there will be various signs that will be visible at an early age. Intellectually sensitive children have been known to start walking and talking at a young age. They even tend to learn how to read before others and generate intellectual growth and capability similar to children much older than them. They also tend to demonstrate a higher reasoning ability and the ability to master skills and concepts with less practice and repetition. But while they may be intellectually gifted, they may often find it difficult to navigate social situations. They can often be highly critical of others and themselves as well. That said, they may require constant encouragement and motivation to overcome certain challenges.

Too Sensual

Sensual hypersensitivity is another form of sensitivity that is commonly seen in children. Hypersensitive children like these tend to have senses that are a lot more sensitive than average. These include the senses of touch, sound, sight, taste and smell. The effect of these hypersensitive senses can manifest themselves in starkly different ways. Some children will become music lovers, being able to remember tunes and lyrics better than anyone else, while others may become picky eaters, often not liking a particular type of food because of its texture, taste, or smell. Due to their sensitive senses, they can often experience sensory overload and may require some time to recover. This can often become a problem for them as they can get bothered and overwhelmed by loud noises, bright lights, and strong smells. But while having oversensitive senses has its cons, it has its own advantages. Pleasant aromas can become more enjoyable, and delicious food can seem more flavorful.

Identifying if children have hypersensitive senses is quite important to be able to guide them better. Only if you understand the challenges children face will you be able to help them overcome them. It is not always possible to control one's environment, and so one needs to learn how to adapt to certain situations. Highly sensitive people often use noise-canceling headphones to filter out unwanted and uncomfortable sounds and often wear clothes that feel good to touch. By knowing what bothers your child, you can not only help your child learn to cope better. But can also provide solutions that can help them to overcome their challenges.

Imaginative

Most children have vivid imaginations, some more than others. Highly sensitive children often tend to be extremely imaginative. They often overthink situations and tend to imagine different outcomes. Their colorful imaginations often lead to their imagining the worst possibilities, which can cause them to lose confidence and often prevent them from trying out new things and exploring new avenues. But, at the same time, they are also creative in nature and possess a good sense of humor. Imaginative children are also prone to being emotionally sensitive as well and may conjure up imaginary friends. They also tend to enjoy reading, especially fiction and show a penchant for poems, drama, and music.

Psychomotor

Psychomotor sensitivity or rather psychomotor over excitability is common in highly sensitive children. Children that have higher psychomotor sensitivity often exhibit higher levels of energy. Consequently, they move around a lot, indulge in sports more than usual, and often get restless and fidget a lot if asked to sit and remain still. Psychomotor sensitivity in children can often be misdiagnosed as

Attention Deficit Hyperactivity Disorder. However, while they can often display hyperactivity, in general, psychomotor sensitive children do not have a problem with focusing their attention as long as they develop an interest in the activity and remain mentally stimulated. It is also common to see signs of compulsive and impulsive behavior like compulsive organizing, compulsive talking, rapid speech, and nervous habits and ticks like biting the lip. They often also display high levels of competitiveness. While as infants, they may sleep less, even as adults, they display the ability to work longer than others without getting tired. Indulging in sports and other forms of physical activities can be a productive way for them to channel their energy.

Understanding the sensitivities of your child can help you identify the best approach to help them identify their talents and overcome their weakness. Raising a highly sensitive child requires a lot of patience and understanding. But once you identify the nature and intensity of their sensitivities, it can help you become a more effective, supportive, and nurturing parent. To identify the kind of sensitivity your child exhibits, you need to look out for certain characteristics in your child's personality. However, you should also be aware that the sensitivity of a highly sensitive child may not fall into an exclusively specific category. Highly intellectual children often exhibit the inability to understand and read the emotions of others. They can also be overly critical of their peers, making it difficult for them to read social cues. But, at the same time, they can be highly in tune with their own emotions, and it may be difficult for them to cope with emotionally stressful situations. Every child is unique, and to provide them with the best possible upbringing, the first thing a parent needs to do is connect with them and understand their needs and requirements. It is not easy to determine if your child is overly sensitive or spoiled. If your child is stubborn and often misbehaves, there are different ways to help out. Methods like positive reinforcement to motivate them to improve their behavior can be useful and other methods like offering them a choice instead of ordering them to do things a certain way can help. But if your child is overly sensitive, you should adopt a different approach. Being able to accept and embrace the high sensitivity of your child as a gift rather than a problem is half the battle. The following chapters in this book will help guide you on how different disorders can be linked. They will help you understand how you can help your child to cope with different challenges and help to develop and nourish your child's talents.

CHAPTER 3:

IS YOUR CHILD SPOILED OR SENSITIVE?

The ultimate question. It can be difficult to discern between a child who is spoiled and one who is sensitive, as these can manifest in similar ways. Figuring out which one your child is will help you to put their behavior into perspective for your own sanity, as well as to figure out the best methods going forward.

'The Spoiled Child Syndrome' has been developed by psychologists who have characterized certain patterns of behavior.

Here are some of the characteristics of a spoiled child, according to psychologists.

Manners

You may assume that a spoiled child will lack manners in any situation they find themselves in. However, some psychologists disagree with this and have pointed out that if a child is polite with others but not with you, this could be an indication of them being spoiled. This is not because they are intentionally trying to be rude or ungrateful but rather because they take whatever their family does for them for granted. They expect to be treated a certain way and don't feel that they should be grateful for it.

This can cause issues later on in life when the child grows into an adult who doesn't feel or express gratitude toward those closest to them because they simply expect a certain type of treatment. Anything else would be unacceptable, so they don't feel the need to be grateful or polite.

Lack of Empathy

Does your child lack empathy in their interactions with their peers? If your child does not understand that they can't expect something from others without giving something in return, this indicates a lack of empathy on their part. This leads to selfish behavior as your child is unable to connect with others, and their peers will feel uncomfortable and will eventually stop wanting to play with or be friends with your child.

If you notice this pattern in your child's interaction with others or that their peers appear to distance themselves from your child, this could indicate spoiled tendencies. Of course, you must approach this with some nuance. A child not wanting to share is not always an indication of being spoiled but rather that they cannot comprehend why they would need to do so. Take into account their age and cognitive abilities. Forcing your child to share won't automatically unravel spoiled tendencies but could lead them to eventually believe that they should expect their toys to be snatched away from them without a moment's notice. This could lead to other behavioral issues further down the line.

Tantrums

Does your child throw tantrums when they don't get their own way? Most people would remark that a child is spoiled if they throw tantrums every time they don't get their way. However, this is not always the case. If your child is emotionally unregulated or is unable to express their emotions, they may express themselves by throwing a tantrum. Throwing a tantrum could be their way of trying to communicate something to you, or they may be tired and frustrated from not being able to communicate their emotions effectively, leading to a meltdown.

You may become frustrated with these outbursts because, to you, it doesn't seem like anything has gone majorly wrong. However, for a child who cannot communicate their emotions effectively, a slight frustration could be the straw that broke the camel's back. It's normal for children to be disappointed and express this if they are told no. In fact, you probably do this sometimes too. If the tantrums are fairly often or happen every time they are denied something, this is a sign something could be wrong here.

If your child has reached an age where they can and are communicating effectively, then throwing tantrums at any inconvenience could certainly be a form of manipulation. Perhaps they have figured out that throwing one gets you to give in to them, or they get their way a lot easier. If your child ends up getting what they want and seems pleased with themselves, while you end up flustered and exhausted, this is a pretty clear indication of manipulation.

Dependence

All children depend on their parents. This is what you want. Note if your child is extremely dependent on you. Extreme dependence such as not being able to sleep unless you're present or having a fit every time they're apart from you could indicate a spoiled child. Of course, this must be contextualized. Take into account your child's age and their ability to communicate with you. Perhaps throwing a fit is their way of saying that they'll miss you. If they are completely unable to be left alone and are of school age, this may be a sign that they are too dependent on you.

This could certainly cause issues for them later in life as their sense of attachment is unhealthy and misdirected. A child's inability to be apart from their caregiver(s) is a sign that they may not have been modeled independence. Children should, from around the age of 3, assist in small chores such as picking up toys. At around 5, they can help out a little more, and at 10, they can even do things such as helping out in the kitchen.

If your child refuses to do any of these things just because they don't want to, this could point to a spoiled child.

It's normal to have to nag a few times to get your child to do a chore or brush their teeth, for example. If, however, you need to bribe or offer an incentive almost every time they need to do something, this could be a sign of the child being spoiled. A child may have become used to being bribed or receiving an incentive for every little thing they are asked to do. This sets a dangerous precedent as they will begin to believe that they don't need to do something unless they receive something in return. A bribe or incentive may be offered out of frustration or because you don't have the time to wait around for them to do something simple.

Of course, your child may refuse to do something out of an inability to communicate something to you that may have nothing to do with the task at hand. Use discernment and notice if your child reacts like this every time they are asked to do something or if it could be related to something else.

Self-Centered

Spoiled children tend to be very self-centered. They believe that the world truly revolves around them and are unable to see any other perspective. Because of this, they are demanding and bratty just because they view themselves as being the number one priority. Of course, children should exhibit a healthy sense of confidence and self-esteem, and this is great. However, if they become overly confident to the point that they think they are better than others and deserve better things or treatment, this could be a sign of being a spoiled child.

Being self-centered can manifest in others ways, such as a lack of patience. They could demand things in this instance and not comprehend why they shouldn't get them. This is a result of feeling entitled.

Sore Losers

Spoiled children don't usually enjoy games that involve competition. This is because they can be sore losers. Although at one point, psychologists believed that children should be raised in a way that made every child feel like a winner, it seems they have changed their minds. This is because children should be able to learn lessons like losing to others or not always being the winner. This can serve them well later on in life so that they can pick themselves back up after a fall. By making a child feel like they are always a winner, as they develop, they will be unable to understand that it's okay to lose and they will still be okay.

Losing can be a vital part of a child's healthy self-esteem. A spoiled child may refuse to get involved in games where they know they have a chance of losing. This is because they can't quite seem to handle not winning every single time. If your child is involved in competition-style games, they may blame others for their poor performance or be sour towards those who are winning.

Lack of Free-Time

Does your child occupy all your free time? Raising children consumes the majority of your time, which is completely normal. If your child is strongly dependent on you, this could be eating into your free time as well as other family members. If your child is spoiled, they may believe that they are deserving of occupying everyone's free time because they need attention. When a child is spoiled, they can often become the center of the family, and everything will begin to revolve around them. If you lack free time in your life, notice if this is because you're super busy or because your child has positioned themselves in the center and demands constant attention.

Of course, they may need this attention because they need to be soothed or because they feel overwhelmed. If your child appears to have had their needs met and received attention throughout the day and yet still acts out in an attempt to garner more attention from you or other family members, this could be a sign of a spoiled child.

Authority

Not recognizing authority is usually an indication of a spoiled kid. Sometimes parents can fall into the trap of protecting their children at all costs and defending them no matter what. This can lead to an unhealthy behavioral pattern of a child feeling like they are always in the right and don't need to respect or listen to authority. Children pick up on things very quickly, and if they feel like they can get away with something, that's what they'll probably do. If the child also feels like their parents aren't authority figures, this can often leak into the outside world, and they will lack respect for external authority figures.

Because of their feeling of entitlement, they will act out and rebel just because they feel like they can. Acting out against authority figures is not always a sure-fire sign of a spoiled child, though. It could be their way of communicating something or their inability to understand that they need to show respect to authority figures. Perhaps a child has been raised to question everything, or the child needs to feel like they have to understand why they need to do something before they do it. In these instances, the child simply wants to gain a better understanding and is not being disrespectful just for the sake of it. Children need to have set limits and have modeled behavior for them to re-enact in their own lives.

Boredom

If a child is constantly complaining that they are bored or are unable to entertain themselves, this could be a sign of them being spoiled. Most 1-year-olds can concentrate on a task for around 15 minutes, and by the age of 3, most children can keep themselves entertained. Of course, every child is different and develops at a different rate. This doesn't always mean they are spoiled, but if a child is never able to entertain themselves, this could certainly point to them having spoiled tendencies. An unspoiled child will generally find something to entertain themselves or lose themselves in their imagination, whereas a spoiled child is unlikely to do this as they are used to being entertained by others.

Boredom and dissatisfaction can be two sides of the same coin. Spoiled children tend to be or appear unsatisfied despite having all the toys and clothes a child could ever need. If they express greed or ungratefulness over not having enough toys or wanting more, this is usually a sign of a spoiled child. However, they could also be expressing themselves in this manner because they are frustrated or overwhelmed by something else. Perhaps they want to communicate a need or want but find themselves unable to do so.

CHAPTER 4: DISORDERS LINKED TO THE HSC

Hypersensitivity in children has erroneously been attributed to being coddled or spoiled by parents. Or as a result of a bad attitude problem that requires a strict corrective. Until recently, hypersensitivity has not been acknowledged as a condition that requires careful treatment, and there remains a great deal of obfuscation and misunderstandings about it. This is especially true when it comes to other disorders that are most probably linked to hypersensitivity and which end up affecting the child's quality of life for many years to come if they are not provided with adequate treatment. Parents need to be armed with the clearest knowledge possible in order to fully understand how to tackle hypersensitivity and the issues that may come with it. This chapter is devoted to unmasking certain disorders and their links to hypersensitivity, along with a few ideas on what parents can do to improve the situation.

Taming the Anxiety Beast

One of the biggest disorders linked to hypersensitivity is extreme levels of anxiety. While anxiety as a whole is a strikingly common phenomenon for most children, especially these days, kids who exhibit sensory hypersensitivity or sensory processing issues may exhibit intense feelings of anxiety and even panic. As discussed earlier in this book, hypersensitivity stems from the body's sensory system, and it can affect more than one part of the sensory system at the same time. This means it is hugely challenging for children, and they can feel overwhelmed rather easily by it. This issue with anxiety will actually come about in ways that may seem odd to you at first. For example, if the child experiences tactile hypersensitivity, then they will get nervous when you try to make them wear gloves that feel scratchy or when you tie their hair back with a bow that feels inordinately rough to their sensitive skin. Or perhaps the child will become visibly frightened and upset by a loud noise that may seem completely harmless to others. They may even begin to panic. These are the first signs that anxiety may become a dominant force in their life later on. For this reason, some kids who experience hypersensitivity may actively avoid or delay any situation in which they may feel overstimulated and use this avoidance as a defense mechanism.

In anticipation of any event that may trigger or upset them, the children will, in turn, worry and fret constantly - basically, anxiety will eventually overtake them. Through different techniques you will master in accordance with a dedicated child psychologist, you will learn to tame the beast with your child and make them feel understood and safe. Over time, this will alleviate some of the worst bouts of anxiety they may experience. However, it will be a long road, and the most important thing to do in the interim is not to judge them or belittle their intense feelings.

Obsessive-Compulsive Disorder

People throw around the term obsessive-compulsive disorder (OCD) rather flippantly, misunderstanding the fact that it is a serious condition that negatively impacts millions of people the world over. This assessment is beginning to change, and individuals are starting to understand that OCD is no laughing matter, and it isn't simply a matter of someone enjoying cleaning all the time or wanting to have a shower curtain laid out just right. OCD is - as the acronym shows - a compulsion, and it can drive many to act out in ways that are upsetting to themselves and others around them. The condition can also worsen significantly without proper treatment.

As of late, there have been studies concluding that hypersensitivity in children and OCD can overlap. While the former is a typical - if requiring special handling - variant of the human personality, it can morph to include other disorders such as OCD. Since hypersensitivity essentially points to increased sensitivity of the central nervous system, resulting in deeper cognitive processing of emotional and physical stimuli, it can come to include other disorders over time.

As an example - to help make the distinction apparent - a child with hypersensitivity will usually stop and think for a while before assessing the risks involved in taking the next step. Someone with OCD, however, will think in repetitive and cyclical patterns in an attempt to solve their problems. Some of the brain structures leading to cyclical thought patterns are thought to be at least partially responsible for the emergence of OCD in some people since the ways in which they neurologically deal with impulse control and rewards are a bit similar.

While during the scenario of childrearing, the symptoms of both hypersensitivity and OCD may seem inordinately upsetting, the good news is that a few of the elements that come up in the former condition may prepare parents for the latter. With the help of a professional, the child will be able to calculate and think out different scenarios before acting and will also work hard to implement positive cognitive behavior practices that will offset some of the more damaging effects of OCD.

Emotional Reactivity and Attention Deficit Hyperactivity Disorder

Attention Deficit Hyperactivity Disorder or ADHD is a mental health disorder that can engender high levels of hyperactive and impulsive behaviors in kids and adults. This means that children with ADHD are more likely to experience difficulty focusing on a single task or sitting in one spot for a long period of time. They tend to be hyper-aware of their surroundings despite feeling a bit all over the place, to the extent that their mind may run at an intense rate without feeling as though they can slow down. The rush of emotions and thoughts is intense, and individuals with ADHD report experiencing an exaggeration of anything related to the senses. Taste, smell, or hearing are all on full blast, and it often seems as though few things can dull the onslaught of things this bombardment.

In the same manner, like OCD, ADHD overlaps a bit with individuals who are hypersensitive, leading them to experience everything at a level of eleven as opposed to a more sedate pace like the rest of us. A child experiencing tactile or auditory hypersensitivities is prone to developing ADHD since hypersensitivity is an attribute common to people with similar disorders. While people born with ADHD are also hypersensitive to pretty much everything, including emotions and their surroundings, the medical establishment has not made the direct connection until fairly recently. This means many adults who were already aware of possessing ADHD did not know that they were also hypersensitive until later in life. Previously, most people would refer to them as overdramatic or temperamental beings.

For example, if your child fidgets a lot or has an affinity for a particular kind of material and will only wear clothing made of that fabric, they may have both ADHD and hypersensitivity. They will go out of their way to ensure that their environment feels safe and comfortable for them and will not accept any perceived compromise. Due to the judgment they may face from their peers as a result of their preferences, these children are more likely to feel alienated and suffer low self-esteem, which is why it is important to work with a mental health professional early on, to not only diagnose the condition but to destigmatize it. These early steps are incredibly influential in the way a child will be able to deal with the issues later in life.

Processing Information and Dyslexia

Hypersensitivity is typically described as a deficiency in the ways in which basic mechanisms underlying sensory perceptions are somewhat altered, if not compromised. While the brain does its best to adapt to an overload of sensory input when it comes to sounds, images, facial recognition, the utility of objects or words scrolling across the screen, their processing is not as efficient as it should be. When people have dyslexia and hypersensitivity, the ability to adapt to a given scenario and process different bits of information is about half of those who do not have the disorder. Yet again, hypersensitivity is seen as another kind of comorbidity when it comes to issues affecting not only mental health, in the grand scheme of things, but the ability to process information in a neurologically feasible manner.

While researchers are still working on locating the combination of factors that contribute to creating disorders such as dyslexia, hypersensitivity, its prevalence in children from a young age tends to be a major culprit. Children with a reading disability like dyslexia may have a uniquely different brain that processes information in an entirely different manner, and there are a number of overlapping circumstances that can engender the issue. Basically, hypersensitivity can cause children to be less adaptive in accepting information than other children who do not exhibit the same issues with processing. Many studies have proven that individuals with dyslexia possess a difference in the brain's structure and how it functions. It simply perceives the outside world rather differently, which is why it makes sense that those with hypersensitivity would be more prone to conditions such as dyslexia. Since kids with hypersensitivity have a harder time processing sensory input, this dovetails with the difficulty of processing words that marks dyslexia. Sometimes the difficulty with physical motor skills (like walking) or fine motor skills (such as handwriting) is attributable not only to dyslexia but hypersensitivity as well, which is why an earlier diagnosis can make all the difference to the child's life and their ability to do well in academic life later on.

Chicken or the Egg? Hypersensitivity and Autism

Children with autism usually have at least one form of hypersensitivity. Of course, it isn't clear the extent to which one condition informs the other since having hypersensitivity does not necessarily induce autism or vice versa. But, if both conditions were laid out in a Venn diagram, they would definitely overlap.

An autistic child is bound to experience hypersensitivity in at least one of the senses, be it auditory, sensory, and so on. These symptoms can have a profound effect on the child's ability to do well in school, interact with family and friends, or even participate in fun activities. Their responses are not typical of the ways in which normal sensory stimuli are processed, which is precisely why they are associated with the core symptoms of autism, which include, but are not limited to, social deficits or repetitive behaviors similar to OCD.

Chronic Health Conditions

Beyond the realm of neurological disorders or mental health issues outlined above, hypersensitivity has also been linked to a host of chronic health conditions that may affect the child's quality of life in due time. For one, incessant allergies, migraines, sensitivity to fabrics, or other conditions can arise. Given that children experiencing hypersensitivity to their surroundings do what they can to avoid places or situations that make them feel uncomfortable, it may take some time to pinpoint these chronic issues. In any case, it makes sense that kids who are hypersensitive to their surroundings are more likely to develop health issues related to their capacity to process sensory stimuli around them. The nervous system only serves to amplify things that feel distractingly uncomfortable to those with hypersensitivity, and it can whip them into a state of extreme reactivity, causing their bodies to go into overdrive.

These chronic conditions can take the form of feeling pain at even the slightest touch, rashes at even the softest bit of clothing, asthma-like reactions to disliked smells, and so on. Muscle pain and fibromyalgia are also common chronic health conditions that arise from hypersensitivity.

Living with hypersensitivity and sensory issues can be difficult for anyone, especially children since they try their best to communicate their thoughts and feelings to a world that fundamentally misunderstands them. The temper tantrums, crying episodes, and feelings of intense sadness or anxiety are not always taken seriously by adults. But if parents pay close attention, they can locate the issue early on, along with any of the attendant behavioral or neurological disorders that sometimes accompany hypersensitivity.

CHAPTER 5:

UNDERSTANDING THE BEAUTY OF HS IN CHILDREN

Many people think of dealing with a highly sensitive person as something quite intimidating and challenging. Even when you love the person and care deeply for them, having to carefully think about each word and action can be very tiring. Sometimes, even after trying your best, it seems as though you can never get it right. Children, whether they are highly sensitive or not, are all generally hard to deal with. It's totally normal for parents to snap every once in a while, even when they constantly remind themselves not to. We're all humans, after all. The problem is that with a highly sensitive child, the situation can get several times worse. Being yelled at or told off is hurtful for just about anyone, though, for highly sensitive children, these details can strike home much harder.

When you are a parent of an HS child, you can sometimes find yourself unintentionally focused on all the negative aspects. Sure, it can be hard to see the positives when your child bursts into tears every time their clothes are slightly scratchy or when they hear a loud noise. Getting caught up in all these frustrations, however, can easily distract you from concentrating on the overall picture of high sensitivity. A highly sensitive child is an avid observer of the world that surrounds them. This usually turns them into very creative individuals. They can get inspired by almost everything. They get overstimulated by all of these observations, which makes them very sensitive individuals who lead very intense internal lives. Your child is gifted with a gene that allows them to process sensory information substantially more thoroughly and deeply than the average person. It's incredible. An HS child does not merely feel their emotions more deeply, but they are sensitive to the world, meaning that they have the ability to understand it more deeply. What many people don't know is that some of the most influential figures in history, like Martin Luther King Jr., Sir Elton John, Abraham Lincoln, Mozart, and Frank Lloyd Wright, are or were all highly sensitive. Highly sensitive individuals often turn out to be very successful because of their perceptive and creative tendencies. They are also characterized by their acute focus, cautious diligence, kindness, and empathy. This chapter explores the beauty in highly sensitive children.

The Beauty in Highly Sensitive Children

Amplified Emotion

Highly sensitive people find meaning in everything that surrounds them, and this trait can be both a blessing and a curse. Looking for meaning in everything that they encounter makes HSP more appreciative and thankful for everything that they have. It also makes them value relationships, friendships, family, and even material things more profoundly. However, this also means that they are immense overthinkers. This trait can usually lead to anxiety. They may also perceive innocent statements or comments negatively.

However, finding meaning in life is a very beautiful trait that can make them feel grounded and down to Earth. Experiencing the world with enhanced emotions ends up becoming an integral aspect of their identity. An HSP finds joy in the smallest things in life, like the sounds of droplets hitting the windows or the waves crashing into the seashore, which can make their entire day meaningful. Meanwhile, a completely harmless phrase can spiral into a wave of emotional chaos. Through acceptance and understanding, these emotions can be easily managed and controlled.

Incredible Self-Awareness

Being self-aware is one of the most important and magnificent skills that someone could have. Self-awareness requires a great amount of strength that not everyone is capable of harnessing. Self-aware individuals can recognize their consciousness, and they are aware of their lifestyle, body, and environment. They can objectively assess themselves, keep their values and behaviors in alignment and, as counter-intuitive as it may sound, they can regulate their emotions and accurately comprehend how others perceive them.

Highly sensitive children, and individuals in general, are usually very in tune with their emotions and the reactions that accompany them. In time, as they start becoming more familiar with themselves and grasp a better understanding of who they are, they begin to recognize and identify their triggers. Having a support figure in their lives at this point is quite important as they need to learn that their emotions, as intense as they may be, are valid. This way, they will feel encouraged to share the things that overwhelm them and communicate when they don't feel at their best. Accepting that this type of sensitivity is part of who they are can help boost their confidence and foster their self-awareness.

Heightened Empathy

Since highly sensitive individuals can deeply connect with their surroundings, they can easily put themselves in other people's shoes. They can innately mirror other people's emotions, and it happens instinctively. This typically makes an HSP more empathetic than others. While many emotionally intelligent people can choose to feel for others, an HSP does not have this choice. They unintentionally empathize with people. Their emotions allow them to understand and connect with the world intuitively. For instance, you might have noticed that your child is affected by violent movies just as they are by tragic real-life events. Because an HSP can feel for others, they are very good listeners. While many people tend to give advice or offer practical support when others feel down, an HSP is characterized by their ability to listen and provide emotional support.

Innate Nurturing Abilities

It's only natural that these great empathetic individuals will be born with the ability to nurture others. Highly sensitive children may not be as aware of this fact as HS adults are, but an HSP knows that not all people experience things as deeply as they do. However, because an HSP is very familiar with intense emotions, they can often find themselves trying to help others avoid this type of pain. Many highly sensitive individuals have a very strong desire to ensure that the people that they love and care for are always happy. When an HSP recognizes someone's emotions, they instinctively feel the need to nurture them. They try to understand their needs and do their best to provide them with the type of support that they believe is most suitable.

Self-Care Experts

As mentioned above, highly sensitive individuals eventually learn about their triggers. This, paired with their incredible self-awareness skills, can make them experts when it comes to self-care. Highly sensitive individuals seek peace and harmony because they are always in tune with themselves, and they like to, at least, feel comfortable. An HSP knows what affects them the most and to what level. This applies to both the things that bring them joy, as well as things that overwhelm them. Whether it's confrontation or noise, they know when to stay away. When they understand what makes them feel drained and what brightens up their mood, they start to become gentler with themselves and ensure that they feel taken care of.

Comfortable with Sadness

This may come as a surprise, considering that an HSP feels emotions very intensely, but highly sensitive people usually find beauty in sadness. You may find this hard to believe, especially if your child throws a tantrum when minor mishaps occur. While sadness may feel like an overwhelming surge when it first hits, an HSP starts feeling more comfortable with the emotion as soon as they calm down. This is mainly due to their ability of self-awareness. When they feel sad, they will find a way in which they can feel present and connected with themselves. Not only does this serve as a distraction, but it also helps them accept the situation. As your child grows up, they will learn to find beauty in how they resiliently overcome sadness.

Awe-Inspiring Loyalty

As a parent of an HS child, you may find yourself wondering if your child still loves you even after you unintentionally hurt their feelings. One thing that you should know about an HSP is that they value relationships tremendously. It takes them a while to open up and cultivate meaningful relationships. However, once they do, they will dive right in. They are incredibly loyal family members, friends, and partners. Even if you hurt your child, they will still love and appreciate you for allowing them to feel comfortable enough to be themselves.

Why Their Emotions Make Them Excellent Listeners

Highly sensitive individuals are not only gifted when it comes to understanding, but they are also excellent listeners. This makes them great children, students, friends, and it will make them awesome parents, employees, and managers when they grow up. Listening is a skill that everyone needs to master, yet many people still lack it. An HSP knows how to show people that they truly care about them. They will listen, for hours on end, about your day, feelings, and thoughts. This is because an HSP knows what it's like to want to be understood. An HSP does not just stay silent when you talk. They reassure you that they are actually listening to you. They practice something that's known as reflective or active listening. They stay engaged without cutting you off, and they let you know that they accept what you are saying, even though they may not agree with you. They will also encourage you to talk about how you are feeling and why you feel this way. As discussed earlier in this chapter, this is mainly because they have an increased sense of empathy. Because they are keen observers, they can present you with creative insights and intriguing questions. They will not offer you a solution or advice and would rather help guide you through the process until you figure out what's best for you.

While this may not be the exact case with an HS child, the concept itself is very scalable. For instance, if you're telling your child a story or helping them study, don't be surprised when they come up with mind-boggling questions or creative thoughts. An HS child will always try to make sense of what you are saying. They will either feel it and connect with it or find a way to tie it to a concept or emotion that they're already familiar with. This further boosts their understanding, which makes them very smart individuals.

Is the Child Easier to Discipline?

A highly sensitive child responds best to gentle discipline. Yelling and high levels of stress can easily startle them. An HS child also tends to feel overstimulated and sad when they know that they've done something wrong. Among the strengths of an HS child, like thoroughly discussed above, they recognize their triggers and value peace and comfort. Highly sensitive children also tend to have an amplified sense of shame, which already makes them their own self-disciplinarians. This means that they will already most likely have reprimanded themselves before you get the chance to. This is why they will most likely avoid making repetitive mistakes as soon as they learn that they are wrong. A highly sensitive child will always seek your approval. They may always worry about getting in trouble, and therefore, avoid it. Besides, raising a child that is sensitive to noise and stress is beneficial to you. You will eventually adapt to this type of lifestyle and learn to regulate your emotions. Managing your emotions, and avoiding noise and yelling, will reduce your stress levels, essentially making parenting a much easier task. Highly sensitive children typically learn using gentle reminders. You will not even need to yell, use harsh words, or exert effort to get them to listen. When you communicate the rules, expectations, and standards clearly to your highly sensitive child, they will do their best to comply. An HSP is not a risk-taker and has a very strong inner moral compass.

There are many misconceptions regarding highly sensitive children in society. Many people think that being sensitive means that they're weak. However, what they fail to realize is that the term "highly-sensitive" does not only refer to emotions and reactions, but it refers to how they connect with the entire world. Because highly sensitive kids feel much more intensely than others, they are very observant, creative, and empathetic. They also have a strong sense of morality and justice, making them almost naturally disciplined.

CHAPTER 6: DEALING WITH EXTERNALITIES PART 1: ENVIRONMENTAL SENSITIVITIES

Many highly sensitive children have difficulties with the external factors of the world around them. They can react negatively to stimuli such as sights, sounds, smells, tastes, and textures of things both inside and outside the home. Being able to deal with these externalities in a productive way will allow you to keep your child from becoming overstimulated and prevent them from having negative reactions to these stimuli. This is key to ensuring healthy development as they grow, particularly when they're at the age where social interactions become more prevalent in their lives.

The environmental elements that highly sensitive children encounter can cause them to become agitated and experience severe emotional outbursts. It's not uncommon for them to throw temper tantrums or begin crying uncontrollably when there is something that makes them react negatively to a particular sensation. You can deal with these problems using a number of coping mechanisms to reduce your child's exposure to sensory stimuli in the environment and learn how to manage their discomfort with the things that cause them distress.

Why It's Important to Deal with Environmental Sensitivities

It's important that you understand why dealing with your child's environmental sensitivities is necessary to help cope with their behavioral issues. When a child is still developing, the exposure they have to external factors can affect the way that their brains evolve. Overexposure to triggering stimuli can cause problems in the way they respond to their environment. They can establish negative habits and emotional responses that will hinder them later in life. We live in a world that is full of vivid and intense multisensory environments, and the way we interact with and respond to everything around us determines our ability to cognitively process the things we see, hear, smell, taste, and touch. If your child is unable to handle interactions with these things, it will hinder their development and their ability to understand

and learn important lessons necessary to navigate the world around them.

The way your child processes sensory stimuli can also determine their ability to function in social situations. If they become overwhelmed by the things they encounter in their environment, they may not be able to interact with other individuals in a natural manner. Many highly sensitive children are prone to becoming socially awkward, as being exposed to stimuli that make them uncomfortable makes it difficult for them to carry out normal social functions. Making friends and playing with others becomes a challenge for them since they may not be able to interact with the same toys or participate in games where the stimuli overwhelm them. Helping them overcome these issues is paramount in order to manage the development of highly sensitive children.

Controlling Exposure to Sensory Stimuli

There are many ways you can deal with your child's environmental sensitivities. Controlling their exposure to the various sensory stimuli they experience will help to minimize any triggering factors that will set them off. Highly sensitive children tend to become disturbed by loud noises, strong smells, and certain textures of objects or foods. Learning how to manage these things in your child's daily life is key to preventing them from becoming overwhelmed. Talk to your child and observe actions that may indicate these sensitivities.

Limit Exposure to Sounds and Smells

You can limit your child's exposure to the many sensory stimuli they encounter throughout the day. If they're going to be around loud noises, give them earplugs to minimize the amount of sound they will hear and prevent them from becoming overstimulated. You can also get them noise-canceling headphones that help block out external sounds and allow them to listen to music or other sounds that they enjoy. Allowing them to get used to certain displeasing noises on their own terms can let them adjust to environmental stimuli without overwhelming them.

When there are strong odors present, use something to counter these smells with a scent they find pleasing, such as mint or gum. Avoid using strong fragrances around them. This includes perfumes, cologne, or hair care products that produce a noticeable smell. While at home, you can practice accustoming your child to strong scents through the use of aromatherapy, but be sure to start with very mild smells at first. If a certain smell triggers them even in small doses, you may have to simply find ways to avoid them.

Create a Sensory Safe Space

Give your child places they can go in your home that are free from anything that can be overly stimulating. This can be something like a playroom where external sound can be minimized and without electronic devices or toys that will cause your child distress. Simple items with soothing colors and textures can help them to experience pleasing sensations that keep them calm. Toys like soft building blocks or a bin of rice that they can dig their hands into will let them indulge in controlled sensory stimuli that won't overwhelm them. Get to know which environments your child loves.

Control Exposure to Electronic Devices

Around bedtime, remove any electronic devices that might interrupt your child's ability to sleep. This includes anything like televisions, digital clocks, computers, tablets, or smartphones. Even when not being used, electronic devices can give off electric and magnetic fields (EMFs) that disrupt the natural electrical neural pathways in the brain, causing distress to your child. Many of these devices also emit a blue light that will interfere with your child's circadian rhythms, as well as suppress the production of melatonin that's essential for a restful sleep cycle.

Provide Comforting Clothing

You can help your child remain calm by ensuring the clothing they have is something they're comfortable with. If they are disturbed by the seams on their socks rubbing against their toes, buy seamless socks or ones where the seam is above the toes. Many highly sensitive children become irritated by the tags on their clothing, so cut them off beforehand. Purchasing soft clothing like shirts made from 100% cotton fabric.

Create Simple Routines

Many highly sensitive children will benefit from having simple routines to follow throughout the day. In the morning, teach them to wash their faces, brush their teeth, and comb their hair. Have time set aside for them to play outside and time when they can come inside and play in a limited stimuli environment. When you know that certain events will occur that may overwhelm them - with external factors like loud delivery trucks arriving or landscapers using mowing equipment outside - have your child use this time to do something inside and wear earplugs or noise-canceling headphones.

Serve your child meals at set times, so they know to expect the smells and sounds associated with cooking and preparing food. It can also help to have a schedule of the types of meals you give them during the week, such as macaroni and cheese for lunch on Mondays, pizza for dinner on Fridays, or eggs and pancakes for breakfast on the weekends. Make sure the textures of the food they consume do not agitate your child. If they don't like things that are too crunchy, give them foods that are softer and easier to chew. If strong tastes overwhelm them, find mild, tasteless meals like rice, oats, or spinach that they can eat. Over time, reintroduce foods they have an aversion to and allow them to become used to the texture, taste, and smell of the offending food.

Get Started Early

The best way to make it easier to deal with a highly sensitive child is to engage these strategies early in their development. Getting them accustomed to environmental stimuli and setting routines before they've picked up bad habits or negative responses to external factors will ease them into being able to handle the world around them. A child's cognitive development is at its most susceptible when they're very young, so establishing coping mechanisms to help them function early on sets them up for better functionality when exposed to irritating sensory stimuli later on.

Coping Mechanisms in Action

Bob and Barbara have a highly sensitive child named Christian. He had difficulties with loud noises and rough textures, as well as being considered a picky eater. Certain stimuli like bright, primary colors and rapid imagery were things toward which he was drawn. In school, he had trouble socializing with the other students and often sat alone and indulged in coloring in or played with action figures. Bob and Barbara were concerned about his development and began employing certain coping mechanisms to deal with their child. This included limiting his exposure to sensory stimuli and allowing him to become accustomed to the ones that caused him distress, as well as creating a safe space where he could explore his reactions to the stimuli that agitated him.

One of Christian's triggers was the noise of his mother's vacuum. He would become agitated whenever she tried using it, which forced her to settle for less-ideal methods of cleaning. Finally, Barbara purchased a pair of noise-canceling headphones for Christian and would allow him to stay in the room furthest from where she was vacuuming so he could play Sonic the Hedgehog video games with the headphones plugged into his television. The video game kept his attention with its bright blue and red character and quick, flashy gameplay, while the simple, monotonous music in the background soothed him. This allowed Barbara to use her vacuum without causing an outburst from Christian.

When Bob and Barbara made their son food, he refused to eat meals such as grilled cheese or spaghetti and would even go as far as gagging upon seeing or smelling them. However, he would eat macaroni pasta and cubed cheese. Christian liked any food with perfectly smooth textures and edges. Those he would not eat were often labeled by him as "stringy" or "rough." Things like eggs, fish, chicken and cold cuts would set him off, and he appeared to be bothered by their smell as well.

Bob and Barbara ended up feeding him his preferred meals on a regular schedule, which reduced his outbursts when being exposed to the food he disliked. Unfortunately, they could not control what other people at school or in restaurants would eat, which would cause Christian discomfort when around them. They began slowly letting him become accustomed to the foods that triggered him, giving him time outside of meals to play with spaghetti or substances with similar textures to those he disliked, such as putty and shaving cream. While he still did not want to eat these types of foods, he would not gag at the mere sight or smell of them.

In school, Christian had a tendency to avoid other children and play by himself. He didn't like the loud, rough games the other kids participated in, preferring to color in or play with action figures. Bob and Barbara attempted to bribe Christian to interact with other children by purchasing a new action figure for him anytime he played with his fellow students, but this quickly set an unhealthy precedent where he would put in minimal social interaction in order to gain access to a new toy.

When it became clear this wasn't helping, they switched tactics to something more productive.

Instead of bribery, Bob and Barbara set up playdates with one of Christian's classmates at their own home, allowing them to control the environment in which Christian and the other child interacted. They provided the pair with toys that Christian enjoyed and had them play in a room with minimal distractions. Because Christian was comfortable, he had an easier time socializing with the other child, allowing him to create a connection with his friend. He made a friend that he would be at ease with while in school.

After a few more playdates, Bob and Barbara encouraged them to go outside and suggested games that were more physically active but not quite as rough or overstimulating as the ones other children participated in at school. Once Christian was acclimatized to this type of behavior, they had him work his way up to things like football and basketball. After he became accustomed to the sensory interactions of football, he found he really enjoyed it. Christian ended up joining a Pop Warner league, and later on, even played for his high school team.

By using these coping mechanisms as early interventions in Christian's development, Bob and Barbara were able to give their highly sensitive child the ability to manage his reactions to environmental stimuli. He did not have the problems that some children encountered later in their development when their external sensitivities were not properly handled. They understood what caused Christian's negative responses to certain stimuli and used the strategies available to them to both prevent him from becoming overwhelmed and slowly acclimatize him to the things he would have to encounter out in the world.

Important Things to Remember

There are some important things to remember when dealing with the environmental sensitivities of a highly sensitive child. Avoidance of sensory stimuli is only a tool to assist you in helping your child manage the external factors that disturb him—it's not the solution. Simply preventing them from having to experience any uncomfortable sights, sounds, smells, tastes, and textures will only keep them calm when you can control their environment. But unless you intend to keep them locked in their room their entire life, you won't be able to control the things they encounter when out in the world. A key part of these strategies is allowing your child to slowly get used to things that cause them discomfort so they can learn how to deal with being exposed to them.

Another important thing to keep in mind is that every child is different in how quickly they can adapt to changes. Some will be able to acclimatize to stimuli that cause negative reactions fairly quickly, but others will take much longer to be able to handle exposure to things they dislike. It's a process, so sticking to it no matter how long it takes will ensure that your child is able to thrive in any environment, regardless of the external factors they encounter. Setting them up early on to be able to deal with irritating sensory stimuli can have a profoundly positive effect on how well they perform in school, work, and society at large later in life.

As a parent of a highly sensitive child, your job is a difficult one. You can make it easier on yourself by following the strategies for dealing with externalities and environmental sensitivities presented above. The world is a bright, loud place with many stimuli that your child will be forced to endure, and if they are unable to handle them, it will make both your life and theirs harder to manage. Don't worry about getting it right on the first try—you'll learn what works best as you go. The important thing is that you continue to do your best to give your child the means to deal with the external factors that can be overwhelming, allowing them to prevent themselves from becoming overstimulated and having a meltdown. Keeping them calm will make it a much simpler task for you when parenting them.

CHAPTER 7: DEALING WITH EXTERNALITIES PART 2: RELATIONSHIPS

All highly sensitive children display common threats, such as registering more sensory information and having an overly emotional response to this information. However, as discussed earlier, there are several types of sensitivity your child could be affected by. Consequently, the child's response will vary from one sensitivity to another. For example, children who are more sensitive to emotional stimuli will be withdrawn if their feelings are hurt, while children who are more perceptive to physical stimulation will probably be hyperactive if they are overtaxed. Either way, being overly sensitive can have very negative effects on your child's social life. Sensitive children feel they are different from others, and if they don't understand why, they often isolate themselves. Recognizing the type of sensitivity your child has can help you understand their feelings, so you can, in return, help them to cope. This chapter focuses on teaching techniques you can use to help your sensitive child learn how to behave appropriately in various social settings. With these techniques, you can help your child build lasting social connections and be more emotionally stable in their adult life. You may find this process a little taxing at first, but as you learn to understand your child better, it will all become much easier.

It All Begins With You

If you aren't a sensitive person yourself, it may be hard to put yourself in your child's shoes. In this case, the first thing you need to understand is how your child's mind works. You may dismiss negative stimuli easily, but your sensitive child can't act in the same way. Imagine that you are put in a social setting, and you are surrounded by complete strangers. This can be a difficult situation even for extroverts, as starting conversations with strangers can be awkward. However, you as an adult would deal with it in a mature way and forget about it. Now imagine that same situation, only substituting yourself with your child in the playground. A sensitive child's senses can become overtaxed with all the sounds and the smells in a crowded playground. They will be too busy to concentrate on dealing with all the stimuli to focus on playing with other kids. So next time you are in the playground and your child is refusing to leave your side, try to ask them how they feel instead of just urging them to play with the others. And if they aren't comfortable there, try to find a different activity for them.

Help Them Understand Themselves

A sensitive child often understands that they feel certain things, but not why they feel that way. By explaining their emotions to them, you can help them understand why different feelings occur and what they are related to. You can explain that losing something will make them feel sad or that being tired will cause crankiness. This can also teach them that we all have the same feelings, only some of us on a much smaller scale and that it is perfectly fine to feel the way they do. Ask them regularly about their feelings about their interactions with others. No matter what those feelings are, don't forget to validate them. Remember, for your child, you are their most important role model. If they feel accepted by you, they will also learn to love themselves the way they are. This is important because, due to their nature, highly sensitive children are often targeted by bullies. The knowledge that their feelings are not wrong, just different, can empower them to stand up to their bullies in a calm manner.

Over time, they can even learn to educate others on how to act around them.

Inquire About Their Feelings

One of the traits of highly sensitive children is their ability to process every emotion on a much higher level than other children in their age group. While this is often the root of their problems, you can actually use this to help you see the world through your sensitive child's eyes. Even if you presume your child is too young to understand some of the feelings, you should still ask about them. Your child may be even more perceptive than you are and surprise you with adult-like answers. This way, the two of you together can come up with solutions much faster to any problem they may have. It's a great way to prepare them to deal with similar issues themselves in the future. Just be careful, especially when learning to use this technique. It might sound simple, but the way you perform this inquiry will depend on the nature of sensitivity they have.

Helping a Child with Psychomotor Sensitivity

For these highly sensitive children, sitting in a classroom can be very difficult because they have too much energy. So, let's say your child comes home from school upset and rambling about being reprimanded in class for being too hyperactive. Because the upset only makes them more hyperactive, you won't get any rational explanation from them right away. Engage them in their favorite physical activity to calm their nerves and get rid of that accumulated energy. After that, you can ask your child what exactly they were doing when the teacher scolded them. If they tell you it was hard for them to concentrate on the material they were being taught, ask them why. If they say they wanted to play or something similar, you can reply by explaining the importance of timing and respect for the teacher. Learning not to play when the teacher is speaking to them will help establish their respect for authority. Additionally, you can ensure your child with psychomotor sensitivity keeps their focus in school by engaging them in regular physical activity.

Helping an Emotional or Orchid Child

These types of children not only feel their own emotions in a more intense way but are also affected by the emotions of others. All these emotions can be hard to handle for a highly sensitive child and often lead to emotional withdrawal or depression. With this type of child, you will need to pay particular attention to nurturing positive emotions. Only in this way will they be able to grow up to be an integral part of society rather than withdrawing from it. If you have an emotionally sensitive child, you may find yourself confronted with a child who is closed up but visibly uptight. Find a way for them to relax, and inquire about their issue. One of the most common problems with this type of sensitive child will be their unwillingness to interact in physical activities with other children. If this happens to your sensitive child, ask them how it makes them feel and why. They will explain and feel much better after talking to you.

Helping an Intellectual Child

Intellectual children can be incredibly critical of themselves or others. They will also ask hundreds of questions and won't wait patiently for the answers either. Their nature can seem offensive to other children, which often causes conflict in social settings such as a school. By saying the wrong thing, your child can offend their best friend without even realizing it, leading to a fight between them. If this happens, ask your child to reflect on what they did or said before their fight occurred. Did they say something about their friend's looks? Have they criticized their friend's favorite hobby, book, or movie preference? Ask your child how they would feel if the roles were reversed. As they are already unsatisfied with themselves, this will upset them further, something they are aware of. Understanding how others feel the same negative feelings that they do when criticized could help them to use empathy toward others and forge deeper friendships.

Teach Them Flexibility

When it comes to building strong social relationships, the key is flexibility. This is what helps us connect to people and even understand the meaning of true friendship. However, sensitive children are often so focused on their own wants and needs that they don't understand the importance of being flexible. This is particularly problematic when your child is involved in a group activity with other children. Yet this is exactly the place where they can learn how to adapt their behavior to a social setting and forge connections with their peers. They can learn how to share and even how to lose without being upset about it.

While it's beneficial for your child to find common interests with others, persuading your child to actually participate and interact with others can be difficult. You will need to explain to your child in a gentle but firm tone why they need to be flexible and share the activity with other children. You can also show them how fun the activity can be by joining in yourself for a short while. For example, children with psychomotor sensitivity love physical activities, such as ball games, but they may refuse to play with others because they can't have the ball all the time. In this case, you can tell them the game will be even more fun if they have to find the ball and get it back. Never use phrases like "you must" and "you have to" as these will only create more anxiety in your already upset child. Use only positive and affirmative words they will understand and can handle emotionally. Be firm and consistent, as they won't give in the first time. But eventually, they will see the other children having fun and begin to participate. For younger or more sensitive and artistic sensitive children, sharing their toys and craft materials can also be problematic. As these children are often more perceptive to other people's emotions, there is a relatively simple solution to this problem. You can teach an artistic child the benefits of sharing at home by showing them how happy it makes you feel when they share their favorite coloring tool with you. And when they do the same with other children, acknowledge it and point out how well they acted.

Encourage Them to Foster Friendships

Even after they learn how to successfully make a connection, your highly sensitive child may need some help maintaining friendships. Because they are used to routines, they may find interacting with others outside of it challenging. Your child may get along and even act friendly toward their peers in a classroom or regular activity. But what if your child is invited to the birthday party of one of their friends? There will probably be lots of people present with whom your child is unfamiliar. Plus, the children will perform completely different activities than your child is used to. This will make your child feel anxious, and they will insist on going home. You can offer the child the option to do so, but you should also explain how leaving the party will make their friends feel sad. If you point it out in this way, a sensitive child can empathize with their friends and stay at the party out of consideration.

An even more effective way to help your child adapt and feel less uncomfortable in an unknown setting is by preparing them ahead. You can write down the most common questions their friends may ask them and play a little game with your child. Answering these questions in a playful way will help them have fun, and at the same time, diminish their anxiety as the child will know what to expect. This process is very similar to how you would be when preparing for a job interview as an adult. By learning what to expect, you will perform better.

Another easy way you can help your child forge long-lasting friendships is to engage them in activities with children who have similar interests. If children enjoy the same hobby, there is a good chance their temperaments will match as well. You can suggest to them a certain activity, but make sure your child is the one who makes the final decision. This will probably depend on the nature of their sensitivity and the activity level they are comfortable with. Are they into sports, books, or arts? You will only know if you ask your child. In any case, if a sensitive child doesn't feel forced into an activity, they will be more relaxed and willing to interact with their friends.

If you see your child is particularly agreeable to spending time with one or two of his friends, try to partner them in games to give them a little more push. Or you can ask your child if they want to invite the friend over more often. Spending more time together can help your child bond with the friend in a more meaningful way. Doing this can also teach a sensitive child the meaning of true friendship. They can learn how important it is to always be there for another human being, whether physically or emotionally. Make sure you explain to your child how the friendship depends on their behavior as well. They need to understand that even if they can't express themselves correctly, they can be attuned to their friend's feelings. Whether the friend feels happy or sad, your child should know how to act accordingly. And if your sensitive child has a fight with a friend, ask them how they feel about it. Don't dismiss these feelings, but tell them that it is perfectly normal to have disagreements, and what's important is that they feel happy when spending time with a friend.

What You Shouldn't Do

Rush Their Learning Process

Although they are highly perceptive and prone to learn quickly, sensitive children can only learn a limited amount of new social skills in a short period of time. In order to learn a more extensive set of skills, they will need more time, and they will need to know they have it. While little pushes in the right direction can be beneficial, rushing a highly sensitive child's learning process is never a good idea. Rushing could make them feel as if they are doing things wrong all the time, something you will never want them to feel.

Use Bribery or Threats

Using bribery or threats while trying to discipline your child is never recommended, whether the child is sensitive or not. For one, this type of negative reinforcement technique can make them feel like something is wrong with them, which is already a problem in itself. But most importantly, this could teach your child the wrong values in life. Because they go against positive moral conduct, these values will prevent them from forging new friendships and can alienate the ones they have already made.

Make Too Many Changes

Highly sensitive children are creatures of habit, and they don't like sudden changes and surprises. They usually have enough to deal with because their nervous system is often overstimulated as it is. Because they are so familiar with their surroundings, sometimes even the smallest things such as moving a piece of furniture can make your child upset. Try to stick to the same routine and environment for as long as possible in a child's life. Avoid throwing surprise parties for them, and if you do it for their sibling, make sure your sensitive child knows about it ahead of time.

CHAPTER 8: DEALING WITH EXTERNALITIES PART 3: TYPICAL ROUTINES

Highly sensitive children experience everything in their day-to-day life more vividly. For them, even the tiniest sensory stimulus can be overwhelming, let alone more significant changes happening frequently. They crave consistency and having a well-established routine can make their lives much easier. Knowing ahead what's going to happen and what they can expect from every situation can help stabilize their emotions. While they are in school, sensitive children are engaged in activities they are familiar with, which they usually enjoy. What parents often struggle to comprehend is that sensitive children need to have the same set structure outside of school hours too. The daily life of a highly sensitive child needs to be planned from the time they wake up until they go to bed. While older sensitive children inevitably face more changes in their day-to-day lives, they are also more emotionally mature and can deal with them.

On the other hand, younger, highly sensitive children in their formative years need an established schedule. It's essential to set a routine as early as possible in your child's life to help them cope with their sensitivity. This chapter highlights the importance of routines in your sensitive child's life and the techniques you can implement to help your child's emotional development. Planning your child's whole day out for years may sound like a tiresome task to deal with, but it will save you and your sensitive child from a lot of unnecessary stress. As a result of that, your child will grow up to be a much healthier and happier individual.

The Importance of Daily Routines

When confronted with something unfamiliar, overly sensitive children often get upset. Your child might not show it right away, but the tension changes create in them will grow and can mean that they are anxious for hours or even days. As a parent of a sensitive child, you have probably encountered a scenario where by the time evening arrives, your child may have been struggling to fall asleep. Despite being exhausted, a sensitive child can have too much anxiety to sleep if they have an issue they can't resolve. And it doesn't have to be an unexpected event either, as sometimes even planned changes could be too taxing for a sensitive child. But with a consistent schedule, you can minimize the chances of your sensitive child getting a surprise that can overtax them emotionally. Whether their days are filled with small or big events, the important thing is that they are there every day. When they are consistent, everyday activities can bring a sensitive child the comfort of familiarity even if something unexpected does happen.

Developing Plans Together

Highly sensitive children not only require a consistent daily schedule, but they also need to have reassurance about it. Using daily and weekly planners is a perfect way for your child to keep up with their routine. A colorful planner spreadsheet in a visible place can be the constant reminder your child needs to reassure them that everything is as it should be. However, you will need to make sure that your child is comfortable enough with their routine. Go over the plans with your child every weekend for the next week, activity by activity. If there is an event that's not part of their usual routine, explain it to your child in detail.

Some things, such as school-related events, you can't change, but the ones you can will benefit your child. Never make plans that could bring surprises for your sensitive child, and try to include them in planning weekend and holiday activities as much as possible. An excellent way to help your child adapt to these plans is to get them to write down those plans themselves. If your child is the creative type, you can help them channel their sensitivity into designing a DIY planner. It could be a great outlet for your child's emotions, and you will get to understand them better. Plus, doing a fun project like this together could be a great bonding opportunity for you and your child.

Typical Routines

Morning Schedule

To make your child's morning routine go as seamlessly as possible, try to get ready as much as you can the evening before. By preparing everything in advance for those busy school mornings, you can avoid a stressful situation, such as looking for gym shoes at the last minute. A situation like that could make any parent tense, and if you have an emotional child, the last thing you want is for them to pick up on your anxiety. Every evening before going to bed, get your child to choose the clothes they are going to wear the next day so you can lay them out for the morning. You should also check for whatever they will need to take to class the next day to make sure everything is in their bag. This way, you can avoid the morning battles over clothes and focus on serving your child a nutritious breakfast.

Breakfast is always the most important meal of the day for children, and more so if they have sensory sensitivity. Because their nervous system works overtime, it burns a lot more energy even at night, which will need to be replenished. To do that, you will need to make sure your child has the most nutritious and filling meals possible, beginning with breakfast.

Brushing teeth is another morning routine most parents of highly sensitive children struggle with. Whether it's because of sensory aversion or because the child is too occupied with other things, they seem to neglect this important task. If you are dealing with a sensory aversion, a vibrating toothbrush designed for sensitive gums could be of great assistance. Otherwise, you will need to find a way to persuade your child to make brushing teeth part of their routine.

School Hours

If your sensitive child is well adapted to the school environment, they will be happy to go there every day. Even if they are equipped to handle children with sensory sensitivities, not every school will be appropriate for your child. You will need to find what makes it easier for your child to adapt to a school environment and choose a school according to the child's needs. The nature of your child's sensitivity influences this and finding the right school could take some time. For example, intellectual children often struggle with school assignments because they are not challenging enough to keep their minds occupied. On the other hand, some children are not too keen on participating in sports and other group activities. The school should be able to accommodate your child's needs both physically and mentally.

The teachers and caregivers will have to work together to create an environment a child enjoys and where they can express their emotions. While their main focus should be on the materials they are teaching, teachers should also be able to notice when things are getting too much for a child. A sensitive child should be allowed to remove themselves from a situation they aren't comfortable in and reorganize their thoughts and emotions by being alone. This is one of the main characteristics you should be looking for when looking for school or childcare from an early age.

After School Activities

As a part of their daily routine, the hours they spend after school should be filled with activities your sensitive child enjoys. Here you can include anything from playdates to sports or art class and even household chores. The type of activity should be chosen by the child as their preference will depend on the nature of your child's sensitivity. If you already know what type of activities your child prefers, you can encourage them to try a similar one, but don't force it if they don't want to.

It's usually recommended to have only one or two activities planned per day. More than that can have a negative effect on their nervous system even if they aren't aware of it at the time. If your child's playtime involves a group activity, schedule that for one day of the week and a playdate or other social events for another day. Try persuading them to do household chores if they still have free time. If you make it fun enough and do it together, they will enjoy helping you.

It is also important to make time for their homework and other school assignments. Some children struggle to do schoolwork outside of school because they are in a different setting. Try to create a calm environment so they can concentrate and don't rush them.

Mealtimes

Mealtimes can be stressful as children with certain types of sensitivities can be really picky eaters. If your child has a sensory food aversion, you can try a couple of techniques to get them to try new food. You can include them in the process of preparing the food and only use textures they like. All this could make your meals go much smoother so you can fill up your child with healthy food without too much drama.

Even if your child isn't a picky eater, they may still have a problem sitting still and finishing their meals properly. They are often focused on something else, so try to eliminate all the distractions, such as having the TV turned on during mealtimes. Instead of that, have regular meals with the whole family. This could be a great bonding experience for everyone, and it can also set an example for your child on how to behave at the table.

Another reason your child refuses to eat could be that they aren't hungry enough. Keep their meals far apart so the child will get hungry, and don't let them eat sugary treats or drink sugary drinks shortly before meals. If any kind of treat is given, it should only happen after a child has finished their main meal in a set amount of time. This will further establish their sense of routine and help them learn how to adapt their behavior.

Bedtime Routine

Sometimes sensitive children are too wired to even fall asleep, let alone have an entire night of restful sleep. They may be upset for some reason, or they may be just anxious about staying in a dark room alone where their mind races to process all the stimuli they faced during the day. Or it might be because they know each morning brings new challenges. Either way, if your child doesn't have enough sleep, you will have a much harder job preparing them in the morning. The key to avoiding bedtime struggles is to have a consistent routine that starts early enough, so the child doesn't feel rushed. Starting as early as an hour before the actual bedtime could give you ample time to get your child ready and solve any problems they might have.

As their minds often rob them of the choice of responding to a stimulus, feeling in control is very important for sensitive children. Letting your child decide the order they want to do things before going to bed is another great way to get them to cooperate and feel understood. Never force your child to tell you about their day. If you see they are anxious, prepare them a relaxing bath and read them a story. You can also listen to their favorite music together or do whatever your child prefers to do. After their mind unwinds, they will be much likely to open up about their emotions. Or, if your child is more comfortable with it, get them to write everything down in a personal journal. It can also help identify their feelings and take control of them.

Weekends and Holidays

Most people can't wait for the weekend or holidays to finally relax after hard days at work. However, highly sensitive children usually have a lot of excess energy due to their nervous system being stimulated all the time and can't just relax by doing nothing. Besides this problem, these children need the reassurance of a set structure even during the weekends. Their mealtimes and bedtime should be kept the same as they are during school nights, even if they want to change it. Your child may be excited to watch a movie with you and stay up late, but the change in their sleep pattern will make them irritable and upset the next day. You can establish a ritual that you only do on weekends, but only if it doesn't disrupt the week's routine. For example, fun family activities on Sundays can become something your child looks forward to because they will be familiar and know it only happens on that day.

Celebrating holidays with a large family can be very overwhelming for a sensitive child. If you plan to invite family members your child rarely sees, always warn your child about it. You should also inform the family members about your child's nature and ask them to keep surprises to a minimum. Don't let the family influence the child to stay up late or eat foods they are unfamiliar with. They may be tempted to give your child sugary treats, which is never a good idea. The nervous system of a sensitive person is already overstimulated, and consuming a large amount of sugar can make everything worse. When a larger number of people are present, always ask your child if they are comfortable with the crowd and if they aren't, let the child leave the room for a little bit. Leaving all that sensory stimuli behind will help reduce their anxiety levels and lower the possibility of a meltdown.

Coping with Changes

Despite your best efforts, sometimes changes will be inevitable, and you will have to teach your sensitive child how to deal with them in a healthy way. Any change in the well-established routine can create a problematic situation that can escalate rapidly. For example, it may happen that the parent who usually picks up the child from school can't make it, so the other parent shows up to pick up the child. This change makes the child very upset and even angry with the parents. When this happens, you will need to calmly but firmly explain to your child what happened and why it happened. Highly sensitive children are often very empathetic toward other people's feelings. If they understand that the change was better for someone else, they can accept it more rapidly.

You can also prepare your child to cope with changes easier by teaching them flexibility.

There are numerous situations in life where you can apply this method and highlight the benefits of flexibility. Getting ready in the morning could be the perfect example of that. Some sensitive children are more comfortable wearing open shoes that are only suitable for nice weather. When it gets cold outside, your child could simply refuse to wear closed shoes because they are unfamiliar. Instead of forcing your sensitive child to wear them, tell them that despite loving open shoes yourself, you are going to wear closed ones because your feet are cold. Looking to you as a role model, your child will follow your example and put on the closed shoes themselves.

CHAPTER 9:

MELTDOWN TIPS AND TRICKS

Highly sensitive children have intense energy and, of course, are highly sensitive to the environment around them. Thus, a stressor that does not have a noticeable effect on a child that is not highly sensitive can overwhelm a highly sensitive child and may cause a tantrum. To avoid these meltdowns and tantrums, parents need to understand the temperament traits of their child, which can vary between one child and another. Some highly sensitive children and introverts, while others are extroverts, so their reactions to overwhelming stimulation can differ. One child may withdraw, while another can throw a tantrum. Parents should understand their children's personalities and temperament traits to help them deal with their emotions and the physical and emotional stimulations that may be overwhelming for them.

Researchers found that there are nine traits by themselves or when combined with others, have an effect on the response of highly sensitive children to different situations.

1. **Energy Level** - Energy levels here refer to both the physical and mental. Find out if your child's energy is high or low.

2. **Adaptability** - Does your child adapt to new changes or not, and if yes, do they adapt fast or slowly to these changes? Also, does your child adjust to new situations or not?

3. **Intensity**- The intensity here refers to how intense your child's responses are.

4. **Rhythmicity** - Do they like routine? Are they predictable and rhythmic? Highly sensitive children with low predictability don't get that irritated when things do not go as planned.

5. **Initial Reactions** - Do they warm up and engage quickly? Or are they slow to warm up?

6. **Mood** - A highly sensitive child's mood is most probably affected by life experiences, and they do not have one mood that is dominant most of the time.

7. **Distractibility** - Is your child easily distracted or not?

8. **Persistence** - Persistence is the ability of your child to complete a task even if there are distractions and frustration.

9. **Sensory Threshold** - HSCs focus more on deep processing than a low sensory threshold. However, they are similar.

Understanding these traits in your child's personality may help you avoid putting them in situations that will be too overwhelming for them, resulting in a tantrum or a meltdown.

As a parent of a highly sensitive child, you need to learn how to calm yourself down before you teach your child how to calm down when stressed out. You cannot help your child if you yourself are unable to calm down and take control of your feelings and frustration. If a child throws a tantrum and you lose your temper as a reaction to their anger, you will never succeed in calming them down. On the contrary, you will add more pressure on your child.

It is crucial to understand that the fear that caused this tantrum is in your child's brain, and you cannot argue that with them while they are having an outburst. Parents of highly sensitive children have to be careful about what they say to their children during a tantrum, as many of the things said by parents that seem rational and smart to them actually hurt their children more. There is a general rule taught to clinical psychologists when they face an emergency. It is to "do no harm." In other words, just stand there and do not do anything.

Now that you know that staying calm and not saying anything unless you know very well after asking a specialist that this is the right thing to say at this moment let us talk discuss how you can manage when your child is throwing a tantrum.

1. Validation

Validate your child's feelings. You do not have to agree with them, but you need to show empathy. For example, if your child is throwing a tantrum because he/she doesn't want to go to a birthday party, avoid statements like, "But you love your friend! You are just not in the mood today." Instead, you can say things that will validate their feeling right now without sending a message that you agree with him or her, like, "You don't want to attend this birthday party today, and you feel like you are having a bad day." This way, you link what your child said with the present moment and their feelings. Never become dismissive because your child will resort to more screaming and anger to make you see and feel how distressed they are.

2. Patience and Understanding Are Key

Remember that your child is not doing this on purpose as they cannot help it. For example, you can't blame a kid with speech delay for not saying clear words. The same applies in that you can't blame a highly sensitive child for being very sensitive! Instead, tell yourself that your child is doing his or her best and show compassion. This way, you can help your child when having an outburst. However, it will take some time, so you need to be patient.

3. Listen and Repeat

Sit quietly with your child, and tell your child that you are listening carefully to him or her, and repeat what they are saying. It is very important that you don't raise your voice. You need to speak quietly and slowly.

4. Remind Yourself that Anxiety Will Rise and then Fall

Too much talking and arguing at this moment can make things worse. Remember that anxiety will rise, and that is normal, but it will subside eventually. Your role as a parent is to control the situation, so it doesn't get worse than it already is. Criticizing and arguing with a child while having a tantrum will escalate the situation and send the child to more peaks of anger and anxiety.

5. Treating High Anxiety Isn't Spoiling

Remember that punishing highly sensitive children for having tantrums does not and will not work. Actually, it is unfair and harsh and can harm them. Do not listen to others or this little voice inside of you that might tell you that you are spoiling your child and validating bad behavior. Your child is highly sensitive, rather than being difficult. What you are doing is treating their high anxiety using the right approach for them.

6. Be a Role Model

Everybody gets upset during a tantrum, and that includes parents and children. However, parents should be role models and show their children how to calm down. To calm yourself down, do breathing exercises, and while doing so, your child may decide to join you. Focusing on self-control will also keep you away from being coercive and harsh while your child is having a tantrum.

7. Try Distracting Your Child

When the tantrum intensity starts to decrease, consider distracting your child by sharing a story about a time you used deep breathing techniques to calm yourself down, for example. Since tantrums can be associated with shame, telling your child stories about when you yourself needed to work on yourself before calming down can alleviate the sense of shame as they learn that they are not the only ones who get angry and need to learn how to calm themselves down sometimes.

Earth Elements

Our nervous systems resort to Fight or Flight mode when we enter emotional states like anger, stress, and anxiety. It is how our body defends itself against what we perceive as a threat, even if it is not a real threat like in the case of a panic attack. Fight or Flight response is our body's defense mechanism to stay alive. The Four Elements exercise is a calming exercise that can take only a few minutes but can help a person going through these strong emotions. The Four Elements exercise can take an anxious person out of the Fight or Flight mode and allow their brains to make rational decisions. However, it is better to practice the grounding exercises when calm, too. This way, it will come naturally when a person is highly stressed.

The four elements are Earth, Water, Air, and Fire. Each one of these elements helps in a way to make a person calmer. This exercise can be done while the eyes are closed or open in case that person doesn't feel safe or comfortable when closing his or her eyes.

Earth

Earth is for grounding and feeling safe in the present moment. Take a few moments to feel your feet on the ground and the support of the chair you are sitting on. Then open your eyes and find three items around you that you didn't notice before. Focus on the sounds, smells, and tastes that are present in that moment.

Water

Water is for relaxation. When our bodies enter the fight or flight mode, our body systems that are not necessary for our survival at that moment slow down, including the digestive system. When the digestive system is reactivated, our body's relaxation response starts working again. To activate the digestive system, you can make saliva in your mouth and swallow a couple of times. If that is not possible, take a sip of water or suck on hard candy.

Air

Air is for centering. Put your hands on your stomach, and imagine there is a balloon in it. Breathe in to the count of 4, and feel the balloon fill up with air. Hold your breath to the count of 6. Breathe out to the count of 8, and feel the air escaping out of it. You can change these numbers to whatever count you can manage. However, it should be a little bit out of your comfort zone.

Fire

Fire is for imagination. Imagine a place or any activity that makes you feel calm and safe. Focus all of your senses into this experience, and notice your emotions and everything you see, hear, smell, taste, and feel.

When you are done, open your eyes, if they were closed, and get back to the present moment. Notice how you feel, your state of mind, and your breath.

Remember that High Sensitivity is not an illness or a disorder, so there is no medical diagnosis for it. You can talk to a child therapist or a psychologist to help you better understand your child's high sensitivity, but if that is not possible, you can read more about it or watch TED talks that tackle this issue. Observe your child and recognize his or her personality traits to know how to support them. Keep educating yourself by every possible means about high sensitivity so you can make sure that your child is a highly sensitive child and accommodate for their needs.

Always remind yourself that highly sensitive children are unique and special. They have what other children don't, and they are more connected to their environment.

In general, raising children is a difficult task, and raising a highly sensitive child is a little bit more challenging simply because they feel things on a deeper level. However, highly sensitive children are unique and talented. When you really think about it, high sensitivity is a positive trait. You just need to understand how to organize and support the deep emotions of your child then teach him or her how to do that. Here are some points that would make it easier for you as a parent to discipline your child.

- Your child is a separate human being to you. He or she has different feelings and thoughts. Thus, sometimes they get upset about the choices we make for them. Validate their feelings and show understanding without becoming defensive.

- Show compassion with words. Never walk away from your child when they are upset and throwing a tantrum, as this will make them feel unaccepted. Talk to your child and tell them that you can see that he or she is angry. Explain that you want to hear why he or she is angry with you. Create a secure, unbreakable bond between you and your child that he or she knows will be there even in challenging moments by being present physically and emotionally for them.

- After providing emotional support, it is time to set boundaries. Directive discipline is very important when raising a highly sensitive child. Provide consequences to their actions and be consistent. However, you need to make sure they do understand what they did wrong and the consequences of their actions to learn from it. Use open communication with your child, and show them that you are always on their side, even when you have to say "no" sometimes. Explain to them that this is your job, and it is a hard job because when you say "no," you know they will get upset, and you want them to be happy. However, you have to do so to keep them safe.

- Set the tone of your voice. It is not easy to use a warm, calm tone when you are disciplining your child, but you have to do that because our children react to our tone and our words. It is not easy, but you need to stay leveled and calm to set your child's nervous system at ease.

Being a highly sensitive child can be difficult for them because their classmates may label them as too sensitive or difficult and inflexible. Moreover, their teachers may accuse them of not paying enough attention. Feeling different and having different reactions to the world around them could upset them. However, to make it easier for a highly sensitive child to blossom into a happy adult, they need to:

- Learn how to recognize their feelings and emotions and understand that all of the distressing feelings they experience sometimes are not permanent.

- Exercise well, sleep well, and talk to someone they trust or their therapist about their problems.

- Understand that they are perfectly fine. They just have different reactions to their surroundings, and you need to understand that being extra sensitive is actually a positive trait.

- Let their friends, teachers, and family members know that a loud environment overstimulates them, and tell them how they cope with these situations. For example, tell their friends that sometimes they will step outside for a couple of minutes because there are too many bright lights around them.

If you are a parent or a teacher of a highly sensitive child, then you are raising or educating a unique child who is empathetic, connected to nature, and aware of the world's injustices. This child cares about the suffering of other beings. Be proud of your child or student and help him or her embrace their sensitivity and organize their emotions and thoughts. Highly sensitive children may throw tantrums, and their intensity varies according to their age, maturity level, temperament, and the way they communicate their feelings. However, you can avoid as many tantrums and meltdowns as possible when you understand the true nature of your child and avoid putting them into situations that will overstimulate them. When tantrums occur, you need to stay calm and take control of the situation. Being a parent or a teacher is a very challenging job, but it is also very rewarding when you provide your children or students with the support and love they need.

CHAPTER 10: DISCIPLINING A HIGHLY SENSITIVE CHILD

There are many grey areas involved when it comes to disciplining and raising a child in general. Different people have different opinions on how you can get your child to behave. Some people think that the best form of discipline comes with gentleness, while others think that some sort of punishment, silent treatment, or yelling needs to take place. You will hardly ever find two parents implementing the same discipline strategies, and that's exactly why raising a child is a challenging journey. No matter what form of discipline you decide to try out with your child, you will inevitably face several obstacles along the way. While this is absolutely normal, many parents start to doubt themselves. However, raising a child doesn't isn't detailed in any handbook. Every child and every parent is different. Not all parents have the same skills, and not all children respond to the same techniques, and every child-parent relationship is different.

Unfortunately, as a parent of a highly sensitive child, the challenges that you experience can differ greatly from the issues that others may face. Your child is different from other children in many ways. This in no way means that other children are better. It just means that some parenting options are eliminated. Let's put it this way; your child is unique- and even gifted. They feel things on a different emotional level, which is why you cannot resort to specific disciplining techniques that may trigger them somehow. This may place additional pressure on you. Not only do you need to be very careful in your interactions, but you sometimes can't meet your child halfway. You will need to become someone who can deal with your child. In other cases, children usually, in time, understand how to deal with their parents to avoid clashes. You are at an advantage, though, as highly sensitive children are typically much easier to discipline. They are great listeners and tend to have a very strong moral compass. It takes a lot of time to understand your child's sensitivity and even more time to finally get a grasp on the perfect way to deal with them. This is why we are here to help you determine how you can effectively discipline a highly sensitive child without hurting their feelings.

Disciplining an HSC

If you attempt to discipline your highly sensitive child in the same way as you would discipline any other child, the chances are that you will end up greatly damaging your bond and your child's self-esteem. Positive parenting, a parenting approach that encourages you to address any behavioral challenges with respect and empathy, is the most suitable parenting technique for an HSC. If your highly sensitive child gets themselves in trouble, you don't need to scold them or put them in a corner. Making them feel bad is not the solution. An HSC is already very self-critical to the point where they will punish themselves. Resorting to traditional parenting solutions will leave them with nothing but sadness and pain, and they will end up attaching whatever message you are trying to convey to their entire worth.

Positive Parenting

You don't need to make your child feel miserable so that they can learn from their mistakes. You simply need to give them the opportunity to fix their mistakes. For instance, say your child broke a vase. Most parents will respond to this type of behavior by yelling, scolding, or giving their child a timeout. This disciplining technique is intended to make your child feel bad, which is unnecessary because your child already regrets their actions. Besides, by doing that, your child only learns that their behavior was wrong. Someone who practices positive parenting, on the other hand, will ask their child to sit down and glue the vase back together. Even though the vase will not be fixed, your child will learn that they need to fix their mistakes. This encourages them to be creative, makes them feel capable, instills a sense of responsibility, and helps them to grow.

While positive parenting fosters confident children, traditional parenting breaks children down. It makes them feel miserable and incapable. Everyone makes mistakes, and tearing your child down for each one that they make will make them feel like a failure. This is the last thing that you want to do to your highly sensitive child - or any child for that matter. This type of parenting affects many children in the long run. Imagine what it could do to someone who is already very sensitive.

Reflect on Yourself

Check-In With Your Emotions

When disciplining your child, reflecting on yourself is one important thing that you should do. You should deeply think about how you perceive or internally respond to your child's mistakes. All parents feel frustrated when their children misbehave, which is why they usually end up yelling. Frustration is a very normal and powerful emotion. Its intensity typically masks other feelings. This is why you should always take a moment for yourself before responding to your child's actions. It's not always easy to remain calm when your child does something bad. Anyone can easily get angry at their child for spilling water all over the floor - it's highly inconvenient. However, is an accident like this worth making your child feel horrible? You will likely forget all about the incident the following morning either way. Yelling at your child can overstimulate them. They need guidance and need to feel confident. You need to set realistic expectations for your child so that they can feel connected to you. Before yelling, take a step back and clear your head. The best way to respond to this situation is by asking them to be careful next time and guide them toward cleaning up their mess.

Make Them Feel Safe

When they feel connected to you and understand that they can count on you for guidance, your children will feel encouraged to share with you in the future. As they grow up, many children would rather ask anyone else for help if they do something wrong rather than asking their own parents. This is because they know that instead of helping them find a solution, they will continue to reprimand and criticize them. Overly strict and critical parents can lead their children to lie and hide things from them. This is not because their children are bad, but because they end up feeling scared of the reaction of their parents.

Change Your Outlook

If the first thoughts that cross your mind are that your child is either being disrespectful or is just bad when they make a mistake, then you really need to change your outlook. A child who gets themself in trouble is not misbehaved. They are curious and experimental. Surely, they didn't make the mistake to intentionally piss you off or cause you an inconvenience. You should always view these kinds of situations as an opportunity to give them advice, share stories with a clear moral, and offer them guidance. Take it as a chance to connect with your child and explore their world. Try to find out why they acted this way and understand their train of thought. If they were curious about something, try to clear things up and come up with suggestions. This will really help you understand your child and recognize their needs. It will allow you to see your child in a different light and allows them to trust you. It gives you a cherished moment in which you can acknowledge and validate your child, listen to them, and get to know them better. These moments are indispensable; they are not mere inconveniences.

Being a parent comes with endless fears. However, you always need to remember that when your child makes mistakes, this doesn't mean that they are incapable or undisciplined. It just means that your child is human - imperfect, just like everyone else. Try to understand and explore their world as understanding their mistakes from their point of view is very important. You should always give your child the chance to explain themselves, and your focus should always be on the different possibilities and solutions. Make sure you maintain a gentle tone and physical touch when you are communicating with your child. You should always speak clearly and make sure that they understand what you mean. Maintain eye contact and correct them respectfully, explaining to them that by thinking together, you can both become better people.

Love Withdrawal

Withdrawing love when your child makes a mistake is something that can affect your child throughout their entire lives. This type of parenting should never be tolerated regardless of your child's character. When you withdraw love from your child just because they do something wrong, this communicates to them that your love is conditional. They start to believe that unless they behave in the way you want them to, you will not love or even tolerate them. This instills severe confidence issues and hinders their character greatly. People who have experienced this type of parenting tended to become major people pleasers. They are also more likely to develop and maintain toxic and abusive relationships. Your child needs to know that you are capable of loving them even when they don't live up to your expectations. Otherwise, you will be totally wiping out their individuality, inhibitions, and entire character. This will only set them up for a major identity crisis sooner or later. There is so much power in loving your child, and in no way does it encourage them to misbehave. When you express your love to your child regardless, they will not want to disappoint you. Loving your child outweighs any form of punishment that you can instill.

Positive Reinforcement

You should always let your child know that you are proud of them when they have done something right. Discipline applies to the behavior of all forms - the good and the bad. Kids always seek validation and approval, particularly from their parents. Practicing positive reinforcement with your child is one way to let them know that you are encouraging and are acknowledging their good behavior. Only focusing on the bad things will discourage your child and will make them feel like all their effort goes unnoticed. Not only will positive reinforcement help them take on more good habits, but it can also help diminish the majority of their bad practices. Children, especially highly sensitive ones, can feel very unsure of themselves. They still haven't developed the full sense of what's wrong and what's right. If they have been in trouble before, they can feel hesitant even about their good behavior. When your child does something right, and you encourage this behavior, they get very excited. It makes them feel like you are proud of them, which is something that they always seek. Praising your child for good behavior makes them feel confident in their abilities. It also assures them that they are capable of doing great things.

Positive reinforcement will not entirely eliminate trouble. However, you should always keep in mind that many children tend to act out when they don't receive much attention. When you praise your child's actions, they will realize that they can get as much attention, if not even more, from behaving well, than by causing trouble. Instead of being problematic, they will focus on doing their best instead. Recognition and admiration are also great motivators. When your child feels down, using words of affirmation can help them feel motivated to do better. Positive reinforcement can help your child continue learning and growing. They will also keep trying to reach their goals. Supporting your child and letting them know that you are proud of them for trying helps them see things more positively. Parents who only focus on negative behaviors can cause their children to develop more negative mindsets. When you praise your child, this shows them that you care for them. It also helps them to see that you are paying attention to their actions and that you are interested in what they are doing.

There are different ways to practice positive reinforcement with your child. Always making them feel encouraged and appreciated is just one way. You can also give them a small treat every time they do something right. When they do major things, you can take them out or buy them a toy. You should always show your excitement when they accomplish something, as this will make them feel like your pride is genuine and is truly coming from the heart. If your child receives an excellent grade or creates a piece of artwork, you can frame it or display it on your fridge. This can really make your child feel accomplished and will help them feel proud of themselves. Putting their accomplishments on display will also serve as a constant reminder that they should keep up the good work. You can create a star chart that keeps track of all their accomplishments. You can even offer to buy them a gift each time they gather a set number of stars. Lastly, you should always hug your child and express your feelings of love and pride toward them.

Things to Avoid

Besides love withdrawal, there are several other disciplinary strategies that you must avoid when you are raising a highly sensitive child. Highly sensitive children are especially volatile to shaming. Something as simple as "You never get things right," which is a phrase that other children may brush off, can greatly impact your child. You should also avoid teasing your child or making sarcastic comments, even if it's just for fun. Overly sensitive children tend to overthink even the most minor details. Physical discipline is obviously something that you should avoid using on all children. Having a sensitive child doesn't mean that you should be permissive. Don't avoid correcting your child just because you think you may hurt your feelings, as this will not help your child. Instead, correct them kindly and gently to help them grow and develop.

Things to Do

Discipline does not only apply to bad behavior. Make sure you recognize good actions and find ways to reinforce them too. When correcting your child, you can use a sterner voice, as this will help them to understand that their behavior is not favored. Make sure to calm your child down, if needed, and explain to them why their actions were wrong. Always make sure that the consequences are related to their wrongdoings. For instance, don't isolate your child for speaking disrespectfully to an older person. Instead, help them write down a well-thought-out apology. After disciplining your child, you should always restore their self-confidence. Let them know that you are proud of them and that you know that they are well-behaved. This will help them understand that your love and approval are not directly associated with their behavior.

Raising and disciplining a highly sensitive child is not too different from raising any other child. This is because all children deserve to be treated with respect and love. They should all be given a chance to make up for their mistakes and should not be made to feel guilty. However, the only difference is that while some children may not be as deeply affected by harsh words, a highly sensitive child will take them to heart and keep thinking them over. This is why you must be very careful when dealing with your child. Once you allow yourself to understand and connect with your child, it will be relatively easy to deal with them.

CONCLUSION

Even though dealing with a highly sensitive child can be overwhelming for any parent, you can become better at it, just like I did with Teddy. The key to success is all about remembering to stay calm and have a plan of action when they show signs of reacting negatively to a given situation. Show them empathy, be direct, and speak to them in a firm yet soothing tone to help diffuse the problem. Once you've got a handle on their outbursts, you can take the necessary steps to deal with whatever stimuli have caused the problem in the first place. The more you do this, the easier things will get over time.

When you're trying to deal with your highly sensitive child, think back to everything you learned from this guide:

- A highly sensitive child has a nervous system that causes them to experience sensory stimuli much more vividly than other children and feel more intense emotions as a result.

- There are different types of sensitivities that will affect the manner in which you deal with your child.

- You must determine whether your child is truly sensitive or if they are just spoiled.

- Highly sensitive children often have other underlying mental and physical conditions such as ADHD or Obsessive-Compulsive Disorder.

- Understand the benefits of a child who is highly sensitive, such as the fact that they can be a better listener when they're calm and will naturally be more empathetic toward others.

- Control your child's exposure to environmental stimuli to help them handle the externalities they find overwhelming.

- Help your child manage their emotional response with others to foster better interpersonal relationships.

- Plan out standard routines for your child to follow to minimize the number of unpredictable stimuli they will encounter throughout the day.

- Understand your child's personality, triggers, and emotional tendencies, so you know which tactics to use when dealing with their outbursts and meltdowns.

- Take the necessary steps when disciplining your highly sensitive child to ensure any punishments do not exacerbate their behavior and allow them to understand why they're experiencing consequences for their actions.

Taking the Next Step

As a parent of a highly sensitive child, you are already aware of the difficulties faced when raising them. Now, you should have a better understanding of why they behave the way they do and what coping mechanisms you can use to deal with these problems. Try them out the next time your child has an outburst. If you can properly implement these strategies, it will not only make life easier for your child but will make raising them much less stressful for you.

If you've found this guide helpful, please remember to leave a review. I always look forward to hearing feedback from those who are going through the same things I went through when raising a highly sensitive child. I hope you find just as much success using these methods to deal with them as I did.

REFERENCES

4 discipline strategies to use with highly sensitive kids. (n.d.). , from Familyeducation.com website: https://www.familyeducation.com/discipline-strategies/4-discipline-strategies-to-use-with-highly-sensitive-kids

Helping a Sensitive Child. (2001, May 14). , from Familyeducation.com website: https://www.familyeducation.com/school/friendships/helping-sensitive-child

Pace, A. (2019, May 6). Parenting a strong-willed, sensitive child: This is what you need to know. Parentingfromtheheartblog.com website: https://parentingfromtheheartblog.com/parenting-a-strong-willed-sensitive-child/

Parenting a highly sensitive child: Why they don't need to be fixed -. (2019, March 13). , from Motherhoodmaniac.com website: https://motherhoodmaniac.com/parenting-highly-sensitive-child/

Acevedo, B., Aron, E., Pospos, S., & Jessen, D. (2018). The functional highly sensitive brain: a review of the brain circuits underlying sensory processing sensitivity and seemingly related disorders. Philosophical Transactions of the Royal Society of London. Series B, Biological Sciences, 373(1744). doi:10.1098/rstb.2017.0161

Aron, E. N. (2016). The highly sensitive child: Helping our children thrive when the world overwhelms them. Old Saybrook, CT: Tantor Media.

Healy, M. (n.d.). The highly sensitive child. Psychology Today. Retrieved from http://www.psychologytoday.com/blog/creative-development/201106/the-highly-sensitive-child

Understanding highly sensitive children. (n.d.). 5 different types of highly sensitive people. (n.d.). Retrieved, from Psych2go.net website: https://psych2go.net/5-different-types-of-highly-sensitive-people/

7 Signs of a gifted child. (n.d.). Retrieved from Readandspell.com website: https://www.readandspell.com/signs-of-a-gifted-child

Healy, M. (n.d.). The highly sensitive child. Psychology Today. Retrieved from http://www.psychologytoday.com/blog/creative-development/201106/the-highly-sensitive-child

Six things an orchid child needs to bloom. (n.d.). Retrieved from Creativechild.com website: https://www.creativechild.com/articles/view/six-things-an-orchid-child-needs-to-bloom

Understanding temperament: Emotional sensitivity. (2012, August 19). Retrieved from Centerforparentingeducation.org website: https://centerforparentingeducation.org/library-of-articles/child-development/understanding-temperament-emotional-sensitivity/

12 signs that you may be raising a spoiled child. (2019, November 21). Brightside.me website: https://brightside.me/inspiration-family-and-kids/12-signs-that-you-may-be-raising-a-spoiled-child-794844/comments

Borresen, K. (2019, December 12). 7 signs you've raised A spoiled child (and what to do about it), from HuffPost UK website: https://www.huffingtonpost.co.uk/entry/signs-raised-spoiled-brat_l_5defe128e4b0a59848d172c6

Is your child spoiled? (n.d.). Retrieved, from Webmd.com website: https://www.webmd.com/parenting/features/spoiled-child

McIntosh, B. J. (1989). Spoiled child syndrome. Pediatrics, 83(1), 108–115.

Cell Press. (2016, December 21). Dyslexics show a difference in sensory processing. Science Daily. Retrieved from https://www.sciencedaily.com/releases/2016/12/161221125517.htm

Kessler, Z., & Sharon Saline, P. D. (2011, July 20). My hypersensitivity is real: Why highly sensitive people have ADHD, from Additudemag.com website: https://www.additudemag.com/hypersensitivity-disorder-with-adhd/amp/

Parker, H. R. (2019, September 22). Living With Hypersensitivity, from Invisible Illness website: https://medium.com/invisible-illness/the-rare-illness-i-live-with-400be0f6cdb1

Breul, C. (2018, September 13). 8 Reasons Being Highly Sensitive Is Actually a Good Thing. Highly Sensitive Refuge. https://highlysensitiverefuge.com/being-highly-sensitive-good-thing/#:%7E:text=In%20addition%20to%20heightened%20empathy,and%20help%20them%20avoid%20pain.

Make Full Use of Your Sensitivity–Listening. (2010, May 28). Hs Person. https://hsperson.com/make-full-use-of-your-sensitivity-listening/

Mulligen, A. (2019, March 25). Why Gentle Discipline Works Best With the Highly Sensitive Child. Highly Sensitive Refuge. https://highlysensitiverefuge.com/highly-sensitive-child-gentle-discipline/

Prior, A. (2019, August 14). Why Are So Many Gifted Children Also Highly Sensitive? Institute for Educational Advancement. https://educationaladvancement.org/blog-many-gifted-children-also-highly-sensitive/

Schiffman, R. & New York Times. (2020, October 3). "Highly sensitive" children can flourish in the right environment. Star Tribune. https://www.startribune.com/highly-sensitive-children-can-flourish-in-the-right-environment/572612732/?refresh=true

Amy Morin, L. (n.d.). 8 discipline strategies for parenting a sensitive child. , from Verywellfamily.com website: https://www.verywellfamily.com/parenting-a-sensitive-child-8-discipline-strategies-1094942

Brand, I. (2019, January 26). 7 ways to help environmentally sensitive children thrive. , from Greenchildmagazine.com website: https://www.greenchildmagazine.com/help-sensitive-children-flourish/

Dalgliesh, C. (2014, January 14). "my socks feel weird!" morning help for the highly sensitive child. , from Additudemag.com website: https://www.additudemag.com/your-highly-sensitive-child-a-sensory-organizing-system/

McBride, M., & Telzer, E. H. (2020). Why are some kids more sensitive to their environments? Frontiers for Young Minds, 8. doi:10.3389/frym.2020.00113

Schreuder, E., van Erp, J., Toet, A., & Kallen, V. L. (2016). Emotional responses to multisensory environmental stimuli: A conceptual framework and literature review. SAGE Open, 6(1), 215824401663059.

Understanding temperament: Sensory sensitivity. (2012, August 20). , from Centerforparentingeducation.org website: https://centerforparentingeducation.org/library-of-articles/child-development/understanding-temperament-sensory-sensitivity/

Lerner, C. (2020, September 5). How to help highly sensitive children be more adaptable and flexible. Retrieved from Lernerchilddevelopment.com website: https://www.lernerchilddevelopment.com/mainblog/2020/9/5/how-to-help-highly-sensitive-children-be-more-adaptable-and-flexible

Talking to your sensitive child - hey Sigmund. (2018, February 12). Retrieved from Heysigmund.com website: https://www.heysigmund.com/talking-sensitive-child-kathryn-pearson/

Maureen. (2017, November 10). The ultimate guide to friendships and the highly sensitive child - the highly sensitive child. Retrieved from Thehighlysensitivechild.com website: https://www.thehighlysensitivechild.com/the-ultimate-guide-to-friendships-and-the-highly-sensitive-child/

One thing your highly sensitive child needs from you - intentional family life. (2017, May 26). Retrieved from Intentionalfamilylife.com website: https://intentionalfamilylife.com/sensitive-child-needs

7 tips for mealtimes with picky eaters. (n.d.). Retrieved from Funandfunction.com website: https://funandfunction.com/blog/7-tips-for-mealtimes-with-picky-eaters

Maureen. (2018, March 26). How to end bedtime battles with your sensitive child - the highly sensitive child. Retrieved from Thehighlysensitivechild.com website: https://www.thehighlysensitivechild.com/how-to-end-bedtime-battles-with-your-sensitive-child/

4 discipline strategies to use with highly sensitive kids. (n.d.). Retrieved from Familyeducation.com website: https://www.familyeducation.com/discipline-strategies/4-discipline-strategies-to-use-with-highly-sensitive-kids

7 parenting tips for managing the meltdowns of easily distressed children. (n.d.). Retrieved from

Parentmap.com website:
https://www.parentmap.com/article/laura-kastner-tantrum-anxiety-tips

Parenting a highly sensitive child: Why they don't need to be fixed -. (2019, March 13). Retrieved from Motherhoodmaniac.com website:
https://motherhoodmaniac.com/parenting-highly-sensitive-child/

(N.d.). Retrieved from Easacommunity.org website:
https://easacommunity.org/files/Four%20Elements%20Exercise.pdf

Brill, A. (2020, June 1). How to correct a child's 'bad' behavior with positive parenting. Motherly.
https://www.mother.ly/child/practicing-positive-discipline-with-your-kids-is-not-only-possible-its-powerful

Disciplining the Sensitive Child. (n.d.). Creative Child Magazine.
https://www.creativechild.com/articles/view/disciplining-the-sensitive-child/1#page_title

M. (2019, April 2). Discipline Strategies for the Sensitive Child. The Highly Sensitive Child.
https://www.thehighlysensitivechild.com/discipline-strategies-for-the-sensitive-child/

J. (2019a, December 26). 4 Benefits of Positive Reinforcement in Children. Cornerstone Learning Center. https://learnatcornerstone.com/4-benefits-of-positive-reinforcement-in-children/#:%7E:text=Positive%20reinforcement%20is%

20a%20powerful,through%20adolescence%20into%20adulthood

www.ingramcontent.com/pod-product-compliance
Lightning Source LLC
Chambersburg PA
CBHW071418070526
44578CB00003B/603